Design for Dying

DESIGN FOR DYING

TIMOTHY LEARY

WITH R. U. SIRIUS

HarperEdge
An Imprint of HarperSanFrancisco

Harper*Edge* Web Site: http://www.harpercollins.com/harperedge

FIRST EDITION

Designed by Laura Lindgren

Library of Congress Cataloging-in-Publication Data

Leary, Timothy Francis
Design for dying / Timothy Leary with R.U. Sirius. — 1st ed.
p. cm.
Parts of this book are paraphrased from previous writings by Timothy Leary.
ISBN 0-06-018700-X (cloth)
ISBN 0-06-092866-2 (pbk.)
1. Death. I. Sirius, R.U. II. Title.
BD444.L415 1997
128'.5—dc21 97-6846

97 98 99 00 01 (RRD) 10 9 8 7 6 5 4 3 2 1

Contents

CREDITS

We were assisted in this book tremendously by Eric Gullichsen.

Also by Mary Dowd, Michael Horowitz, Vicky Marshall, and Douglas Rushkoff.

Parts of this book are paraphrased from previous writings by Timothy Leary.

Design for Dying

Introduction

BY TIMOTHY LEARY

SOMETIME IN JANUARY 1995, I WAS TOLD BY TWO WISE AND gentle medical doctors at Cedars-Sinai Medical Center in Los Angeles that my prostate gland had become the host of a healthy, robust, spectacularly ambitious cancerous tumor.

It turns out that I am not alone. A cover story in the April 1, 1996, issue of *Time* entitled "The Man's Cancer" placed my face alongside a group of illustrious and infamous men who have recently overcome or currently suffer this malady. Pictured were General Norman Schwarzkopf, Bob Dole, Sidney Poitier, Jordan's King Hussein, Jesse Helms, Jerry Lewis, Michael Milken . . . and me! Rumor has it that 80 percent of males between the ages of 75 and 90 develop prostate cancer. And I'll speculate that *101 percent* of males over age 101 end up playing host to this illness. Before my diagnosis I was unaware of these vital facts. I was also ignorant of the function of this interesting gland, the prostate.

Why was I so ignorant? After all, I am a medically trained psychologist. I have taught at two prestigious medical schools. I have written more than forty books about the human condition. And still I knew nothing about my prostate gland.

The dictionary defines the prostate as "a gland that surrounds the urethra of males at the base of the bladder, comprising a muscular portion that controls the release of urine, and a glandular portion that secretes an alkaline fluid that makes up part of the semen and enhances the motility and fertility of sperm."

What a busy little organ! The prostate is called to duty only at those engrossing moments of male orgasm. It facilitates male fertility. The prostate contributes very little to the plumbing, metabolism, or survival of my body. It serves only a genetic function. DNA has designed this complex gland as a procreative tool for the reproduction of the species, with no regard for my personal health!

These thoughts led to a humbling conclusion. DNA apparently uses me and my body as a lumbering, complicated vehicle to carry around the precious, delicate genetic code locked in my sperm. She (DNA) has cunningly located her fertility and sperm-mobility equipment in a protected and bustling area of my body.

It makes sense, then, that prostate cancer occurs when men age and their frequency of orgasm decreases. The function of the prostate is to squirt out its sperm-carrying alkaloid at the time of ejaculation. Clearly, infrequent orgasms result in a backed-up puddle of precious fluid in the swollen prostate glands of the elderly.

As I puzzled over these spooky thoughts, another emotional event occurred. One of my closest friends, a charming, intelligent, postmenopausal lady, discovered that she had breast cancer.

Since neither of us had any desire to play the passive-patient/victim role, we scoured the available literature about our illnesses. We were charmed to note that breast cancer, one of the most common lethal diseases for women, might be considered a close cousin to cancer of the prostate. The mammary glands apparently play no role in the survival of the woman. They can be removed with no threat to the body. Like the prostate they serve the species, not the individual. It's not surprising to learn that women who do not bear children have a significantly higher rate of breast cancer.

Our attempt to combine scientific fact with rumination about genetics led us to wonder about the mysterious demonization of cancer. I find it fascinating and scary that I had docilely accepted the scenario that the cancer, like communism, was the ultimate "evil" threat to life. Why are so many of us uninformed about this disease?

The answer is obvious: denial/taboo. Most human beings don't want to think or talk about death. The taboo is understandable. None of us primitive primates knows why we're here or where we're going. These issues are scary. Each human being is equipped with a 120-billion-cell brain, but we haven't yet learned how to use it. Few of us are aware of our neural ineptness.

The organized religions have comforted us by providing infantile fairy tales about God and promises of discarnate immortality. Pray and obey, keep your legs crossed, avoid orgasms, and you'll get the one-way ticket to heaven.

But perhaps by making close and intimate acquaintance with our hard-working body parts and by nobly taking control of the operation of our brains, we may be able to soothe our ancient fears with common sense.

Designer Dying

Personally, I've been looking forward to dying all my life. Dying is the most fascinating experience in life. You've got to approach dying the way you live your life—with curiosity, hope, experimentation, and with the help of your friends.

I have set out to design my own death, or de-animation as I prefer to call it. It's a hip, chic thing to do. It's the most elegant thing you can do. Even if you've lived your life like a complete slob, you can die with terrific style. I call it "Designer Dying," and it involves two basic principles by which I've lived my life: think for yourself and question authority.

Related to the many problems one faces in maintining a life characterized by self-reliance and personal growth and anticipating an educational and self-fulfilling death are five challenging questions:

1. Where is personal consciousness located?

Answer: One's personal consciousness is stored in the nervous system. The brain is the hardware—the biocomputer that fabricates and navigates the realities we inhabit. The software systems that operate the brain are a combination of your genetic makeup and your experience—these programs, directories, files, and personal operating systems define the individual soul.

2. What happens to personal consciousness when bodily functions cease?

Answer: Unless scientific methods of preservation and/or reanimation are employed, when the body dies the brain rots. Your personal software systems crash. Your hard drive is destroyed. If you choose to ignore the preservation/reanimation options, there are two ways to deal with your defunct software: you can be passively buried in a coffin and let it rot in the landfills we call cemeteries, or you can be cremated.

Cremation is more dignified than rotting. Cremation is a choice made by the owner/manager of the brain and is approved by the polytheistic-pagan-humanist religions that glorify the individual's gods-within and encourage reincarnation or reanimation planning. The aim of monotheistic-totalitarian religions is to prohibit individuals from exercising any navigational control of conception, reproduction, and postmortem transition. Totalitarian religions prohibit cremation.

Although I'm aware of and excited about the emerging scientific methods for reanimation, I have made the fateful decision to forego those options. I will be cremated, and a portion of my ashes will be placed aboard a rocket ship and blasted off into outer space, where they will orbit the earth before disintegrating upon reentry into the atmosphere. I have always considered myself an astronaut, and in death this will become a reality.

3. How can the hardware of the brain be preserved for reanimation after physical death?

Answer: There are three scientific methods for preserving the brain:

1. Cloning a new brain and body from cells
2. Cryonic suspension of the body and/or brain
3. Biological brain banking—awaiting donor transplant to a new body

I recognize that preserving the brain does not assure that the software directories, the memory files and the personal operating systems, will be preserved. Therefore, the owner of the brain must make arrangements to "save" and "back up" the memory software that comprises the individual's personality and consciousness of self.

4. How can personal memories and genetic algorithms stored in the brain be backed up and stored for uploading into the new or reanimated brain?

Answer: Owners who wish to preserve and reanimate their neuro-memories (souls) must diligently collect and protect material mementos that will help reconstruct the unique personality and personal environment of their lives—within reason, of course. The tombs of the pharaohs are fantastic models of personal-reality storage, but impractical for our times. Material items, mementos, souvenirs, clothes, books, and pictures are obviously vulnerable to loss. Remember the tomb robbers.

The key to software backup, therefore, is digitization. IF YOU WANT TO IMMORTALIZE YOUR CONSCIOUSNESS, RECORD AND DIGITIZE.

5. Success in preserving one's personal hardware (body brain) and autographic software depends on supportive environments and stable, highly motivated caretaking organizations. What are the political-cultural-social steps required to protect and reanimate hibernating brains?

Answer: The basic units for survival during life and hibernation are *in-groups*—small teams linked to other small groups. Intergenerational links are also crucial to keep a system going over many decades.

The following pages will explore these and many other questions and offer a model for designing your own dying. As this is the single most important thing you will do your entire life, remember these basic guiding principles, which have guided my existence and work:

Have a sense of humor.
Conform to the Laws of Levities.
Think for yourselves.
Question authority.
Celebrate chaotics.
Increasing illumination and understanding is a team sport.
Whether it's living or dying . . . always do it with friends!

Introduction

BY R. U. SIRIUS

DAMN IT, TIM! YOU RUINED THE BOOK. YOU WERE SUPPOSED to die on the damn Internet and those CryoCare geeks were going to sever your brilliant head from the ol' cancer-ridden bod and put it on ice. Shit. And to think I wasted fifteen hundred words in *ARTFORUM International* defending the probability of nanotechnology. And I never got called back for another column. Imagine, talking about infinite wealth and raising-the-dead-through-science in the official publication of the East Coast avant-garde art establishment. (Avant-garde art establishment? Indeed. The end of the century is distinguished by quantum increases in the number of oxymorons.) My *Village Voice* subscription has been annulled. I'm lucky I didn't get arrested!

Think of the PR if you'd actually done it. What a media circus. Imagine it. It's 11:30 P.M. Chris and Camella are working the cameras, the CU See Me interface is happening. Millions are tuned in on the Net. The whole tribe linked together with you—the genial, shamanic late-night host of the

McLuhan Age. You say your final words, "Why? Why not." Your sidekick, Baba Ram Dass, pipes in with "You are *correct,* sir!" Those netters who are linked up to a text-only interface respond with -) LOL (thundering applause). Ted Koppel and ABC's *Nightline* assume the best camera position among the hundreds of TV crews doing a live TV feed of you crossing over on the Internet. It's TV about Web TV about life and death and the flimsy border in between. It's infinite recursion—a Mandelbrot moment. Medium rubbing up against medium in a Baudrillardian psychedelic media orgasm.

Out there in America, millions cheer your courage while others complain about the decline of American culture. Between midnight and 12:01 A.M. the phrase *"fin de siècle"* is uttered by 4,583,399 individuals.

The cryonics dudes are there, self-righteously wiping the slacker graffiti off of the preservation chamber and replacing the copy of *An Unseemly Man* by Larry Flynt—placed among the artifacts to be brought along on your journey—with a copy of *The Silicon Man* by Charles Platt. They're just about to remove your head when suddenly the L.A. cops rush in through the front door. Pushing and shoving their way through the crowd of friends, hippies, lovers, cybernauts, technoids, Hollywood liberals, and the fortunately unarmed G. Gordon Liddy, they grab your body, read you your Miranda rights, and cart you and all your guests downtown until they figure out who to blame for this clear trademark violation of the nova heat's control over the Prison Earth "death property." The list of suspects is impressive. Mark Mothersbaugh. Trent Reznor. Oliver Stone. Tony Scott. Helmut Newton. Baba Ram Dass. Eldridge Cleaver. William S. Burroughs. Uma Thurman. But they decide to do what everybody else does and blame Yoko.

It would've been the last great bust, Tim. DUI. Dying under the influence in public without a license.

Or maybe not. Maybe they would have let it happen. You would have woken up in fifty years to a bunch of humorless men carrying clipboards. But hell, I'd 've been waiting in the hotel bar with several bottles of Scotch, a stick of da chronic that'd make your face melt into your shoes, and a whole host of the strangest, slinkiest, sexiest, most dangerous philosophy groupies this side of the singularity. Why? Why not.

Letting Tim Escape Again

-). In other words, I kid. There is nothing in the way that Timothy Leary conducted his last command performance—dying in public—that was anything less than extraordinary. For a year and a half, he challenged the last greatest taboo. I'm not speaking here merely of the taboo against confronting death. There, he joined Elisabeth Kübler-Ross, the Hemlock Society, Jack Kevorkian, the hospice movement, Ram Dass, and so many others in bringing intelligence, sanity, and courage into this still sadly underlit area of human experience. But Leary took it much further. He challenged the *solemnity* of dying. He realized that the ultimate indignity was to have everybody around you lose their sense of humor, to have everybody treat you like a walking *bummer,* a grim representative of the unhappy facts of death.

So Tim designed for his dying to be a party. He said that he was "thrilled" to be dying. He invited all of his friends to come pay their respects *while he was still alive.* When we came to visit, he cheered *us* up. Ever the scientist, he shared openly all of his reports—objective and subjective—about how he was experiencing, and thinking about, the dying process. And while in a condition that would confine most people to a hospital bed, Tim spoke candidly, insightfully, and sometimes even lucidly to the people through the media, granting several interviews nearly every day. Aside from communicating through his words and actions his rare sense of trust in the grand scheme of all things by his celebration of dying, he also communicated an anti-authoritarian message of self-empowerment, of choice and options in how one deals with dying. Leary took every opportunity to let people know that we have choices regarding how to die and, someday soon, we may have choices about *whether* to die.

Freedom of choice. Autonomy. In the end, Tim wasn't a messenger for technotopia. He wasn't a messenger or a poster boy for the cryonics movement. Don't get me wrong. He *supported,* as always, the evolution of technologies that increase our autonomy and our options. He wanted this book to communicate the cryonics option, as well as other post-metabolic possibilities for preserving the brain (which Tim considered the soul), among the many potential designs for dying (and living, of course).

Tim Leary spent his life challenging the taboos that make our public discourse axiomatically dishonest. He succeeded in his own Designer Dying, making it a public celebration and using the opportunity to communicate about personal autonomy and the importance of thinking and being conscious right up to your last breath. And then he made his own choice to escape Prison Earth, not in anger but in love, with his closest friends and family members on hand.

He did a good job.

part 1

LIVING

CHAPTER 1

What Is the Meaning of Life?

What is my life without your love? Who am I without you?

GEORGE HARRISON

If you want to search for the meaning of life you should bloody well bring along a bottle of whisky. At least that way you'll be drunk by the time you start to take yourself seriously.

PATSY, *ABSOLUTELY FABULOUS*

To know life you must fuck it in the liver.

DR. FRANKENSTEIN,
ANDY WARHOL'S *FRANKENSTEIN*

Why be embodied? Embodiment is such a messy solution. It seems to me that this is a problem presented for us to work out.

GRACIE, HIGH FRONTIERS, 1987

Assignment: Philosopher

IN 1962 I MADE A PACT WITH DNA. IT WAS THE standard contract. I was to illuminate, raise intelligence, probe, experiment, and transmit all revelations as directly as possible. I was to disregard ordinary concerns for security and comfort, risk the loss of every major attachment, and accept full responsibility for the consequences. The journey would be the reward—with perhaps an extra special bonus near-utopia on earth and other points in nearly limitless time, space, and intelligence . . . if the scientists, chemists, and financiers could get it together *on time.* As if.

The pact didn't involve a telepathic communication. No channeling was involved. Doggies from Sirius didn't yap megalomaniacal instructions for all humankind in my ear. And if I felt too self-important, the prankster god of acid would provide me a glimpse of my Dagwood Bumstead side (R. Crumb comix hadn't happened yet).

Nevertheless, it seemed that I was assigned to ask big questions such as "Do you believe in a higher intelligence?" and "Is there a master plan?" and "What is the meaning of life?" And to toss off suggestions, notions, theories, eschatologies, and illuminating jokes. In other words, to play the philosopher for relativistic and somewhat nihilistic times.

A millennium or so back, the question of how and why we happen to be around dominated human activities. Europeans spilled so much blood arguing about it that eventually most intellectuals turned away from the big philosophic questions and focused on basic functional humanistic goals, improving conditions for the people. Human rights. Dialectical materialism. Freud.

Take Freud. Post-Freudians are only too willing to babble endlessly about their sexual problems. But asking about their cosmological insights will be seen as impertinent. And should you happen to suggest a possible eschatology in light of the latest discoveries of physics and the Hubble Telescope in the wee hours of cocktail chat, you will likely be regarded as unfathomably weird.

In the 1960s, we promiscuously started raising questions about cosmic consciousness and alternative realities and declaring God lost and found: in a pill, a grain of sand, love, or an Eric Clapton guitar solo. It wasn't just our naïveté that infuriated the "grown-ups." The big philosophic questions had been long repressed and here we were getting all silly about them. To the conservatives, the questions had been filed away as answered by murky, watered-down, mainstream religious dogma. Understand, the currently powerful reactionary religious passions that we would stir up with our cultural shock tactics had yet to be unleashed. For the 1960s middle-class professional, it was more a case of having a satisfactory schoolbook answer available for that rare instance when the question of God and meaning would happen to come up. And to the Left, such questions were a distraction from issues of material suffering, power dynamics, and inequality.

This philosophic malaise persists into the 1990s. Members of Generation X, reacting quite understandably to the New Age philosophic credulousness of the boomers, make it a particular point to puncture all the cosmological and phenomenological hot-air balloons we might care to launch. Still, even Douglas Coupland went in search of God in his novel, *life after god. (R. U. Sirius comments: As I'm rewriting this, Roger Shattuck is on the* McNeil-Lehrer Report *talking about his new book,* From Prometheus to Pornography. *Shattuck, who insists that he's not terribly conservative, believes that we have to learn in the nuclear/digital/genetic age that "the pursuit of truth can be dangerous." The discussion doesn't touch on the phenomenal Orwellian implications of a culture operating according to that premise.)*

A BIT OF CHAOS BEFORE WE START PREDICTING THE UNPREDICTABLE

Now, before I go out on a limb, daring to lightly suggest a possible purpose and navigational direction for existence, let's stare into the maw. Let's have a cold hard look at the facts of chaos. Quantum physics informs us that the visible-tangible reality is written in BASIC. It seems that we inhabit a universe made up of a small number of elements/particles/bits that swirl in chaotic clouds, occasionally clustering together in geometrically logical temporary configurations. Indeed. As complex as the phenomenological world appears, chaos theory has shown us that it's a fairly simple process that produces complex results if it runs long enough. Mathematical philosopher Rudy Rucker suggests that we think of the universe as a simple program that's been running a very long time. As successive outputs overlap onto one another, they build up into a hyperdimensional moiré pattern.

The solid Newtonian universe involving such immutable concepts as mass, force, momentum, and inertia has long been repealed. That dull, dependable, predictable General Motors universe has been transformed into shimmering quantum electronic possibilities. It seems that it all comes down to programs, information, and rhythms—endlessly complexifying with unpredictable results. In other words, John Coltrane.

In fact, the wonderful thing about chaos is its unpredictability. Complex random processes coalesce into approximately repeating cycles. Approximate, but not perfect, repetition. These strange attractors express chaotic behaviors whose rhythms drift. Ultimately, chaos tells us that we can't predict the future with any precision. Unpredictability is inherent in living systems, art, romance, and gourmet cutlery.

Cracking the Code of Life

Still, subsumed within this pervasive chaos is a certain divine symmetry. It gives me pleasure to imagine that we are here to evolve (and *to go,* of course) according to information contained in the DNA code.

There are two prevalent conventional theories of creation. The popular lunatic scientific assumption is Darwinian. Accidental, statistical mutation. Natural selection. A blind, aimless, lurching evolution. We're not just talking unpredictability here. We're talking cognitive void—no meaning extant.

You see, a couple of scientists in Chicago put some ammonia, methane, and water vapor into a jar. They blasted it with an electrical charge and found some prebiotic molecules. And that's it. End of story. We now had satisfactory proof of our origins.

Right. Two and a half billion years ago, a bunch of methane molecules had a party one night with some ammonia molecules. They got bored and invited a few carbon girls over. Everybody started in drinking water vapor. The joint was hit by lightening and, naturally, they started copulating. Well, it's not such a *bad* story really, but we were hoping for something a little bit more romantic.

Now the other theory is that life was designed by an anthropomorphic police-power freak named Jehovah. He's an all-powerful desert-macho dictator who runs around interrogating, arresting, and condemning anyone who doesn't follow his rules or bow down to him regularly. He even stationed an Irish cop named Peter at the gates of his comfortably upscale eternal vacation spot to keep dissidents out.

I find it useful, for the moment, to entertain a different theory—one that resonates with my sense that the universe is on purpose, all about information, generous, big, and sexy. Panspermia.

Panspermia was first suggested by Svante Arrhenius (1859–1927), a Swedish biologist. He suggested that this planet was seeded by spores from outer space. By the 1960s, hope for this theory was already looking *up*. Dozens of prebiotic molecules were discovered floating around in prestellar cloud complexes (clouds of particles that exist before they condense into stars; our sun once was one, as were all stars). They were also found in a type of meteorite called a carbonaceous chrondite.

Then, in 1973, Sir Francis Crick—who along with James Watson discovered DNA—suggested the theory of Directed Panspermia. Crick believes that the planet may have been deliberately seeded. Recent discoveries brought to us by the Hubble Telescope lend still more credence to this speculation, confirming what I intuited back in the early 1970s. It's likely that there are millions of planets on which life exists in our small galaxy alone. Perhaps life on them evolves differently, or perhaps the same process of evolution that is taking place here takes place on other planets. And in 1996, we thrillingly discovered lifelike molecules in meteorites from Mars!

The theory of Directed Panspermia has gained credibility over the years, particularly with geneticists, who don't believe that blind accidental mutations could have taken us from simple unicellular life to the unimaginable complexity of . . . Beavis and Butthead. But, of course, there's no proof yet.

I believe that the key to scientific understanding of natural laws at every level of complexity—the true point of Heisenberg's observation that scientific laws are a participatory sport—is to personalize the events, to experience and empathize with them. It astonishes me that seekers after wisdom ignore scientific discoveries and that reductionist scientists ignore their inner, intuitive navigational compasses.

Fortunately for me, by the 1970s, the message of twentieth-century physics became unavoidable. The men and women who investigate the basic structure of matter and energy reached the same conclusion as the young men and women tapping into galactic central through plants and chemicals. They all speak of the breakdown of macroscopic objects into vibratory patterns, the awareness that everything is a dance of particles.

Physicists started speaking of pure energy and white light. Pop books from Gary Zukav's *The Dancing Wu Li Masters* to Nick Herbert's *Quantum Reality* informed us that the truth is stranger than hallucination, stranger than we can even imagine.

During this same period in the 1970s I dared to communicate what I still believe might be a relatively accurate "readout" of the DNA code's plans for our species. I even published a book, *Exo-Psychology* (later reprinted and currently available as *Info-Psychology),* with the playfully arrogant subtitle "A Manual on the Use of the Human Nervous System According to the Instructions of the Manufacturers" just to drive my many critics to distraction. This DNA transcription was based partly on my trusting my intuitive, high-fidelity receptivity in highly controlled experiments with psychedelic neurochemicals that tune the brain in to receive what seems to be information, patterns, and codes from what has variously been called the genetic archives, the collective unconscious, the Akashic records, Earth Coincidence Control Office, or (your favorite metaphor for cosmic consciousness here). But it was also based on my scientific reading and conversations with scientists in fields ranging from ethology to genetics to information science to ecology to astrophysics, and so on.

Recently, some friends were gathered around the kitchen table imbibing some fine wine and *cannabis sativa.* We were talking, making some light fun of the New Age fad for channeling, when some cynic pointed out that my theories about what the DNA code has planned for the evolution of our species were—in a sense—channeled. I confess. I had channeled my own brain, marinated as it was in the juices of the trendiest scientific theories of the moment, turned on my nervous system, tuned in to my DNA, and read the script as best as I could. So it is now with great feelings of humility that I share with you my readout of the purpose of existence according to DNA. Some geneticists and followers of ethological trends tell me that it looks like a pretty good guess. Hey, man. Nice shot. The theory offers, at the very least, a useful conceit for upleveling your life games and for charting your evolution.

WHAT THE DNA TOLD ME

The DNA code is as old as the life process on this planet. For three billion years, the DNA code has been building improved models of bodies for housing, nourishment, protection, and transportation to the proximity of other bodies which, via physical-chemical mutual attraction, will be induced to unite sperm and egg, carriers of DNA, to create new bodies for housing and improved nervous systems to continue the evolutionary sequence toward its goal.

The DNA code is a three-billion-year-old time capsule of consciousness. The DNA code is the miniaturized, invisible essence wisdom of life. Most of the characteristics formerly attributed to the "soul" describe the functions of DNA. DNA builds more effective nervous systems to pilot, sense, guide, experience, and finally to decode, understand, and spread her unfolding wisdom.

The DNA code is literally a code, a complex message. As I've said, the message may migrate from entities of higher intelligence located in other solar systems within and outside of our galaxy.

It is surmised that these entities seed interstellar and intergalactic "space" with amino acid molecules. These molecules land on planets where, adapting to and interacting with local chemical, gravitational, atmospheric, and radiation forces, they emerge as evolving life-forms already preprogrammed to produce nervous systems. The evolutionary material was already preplanned before arrival on this planet to evolve bilateral, serially imprinting nervous systems that can master planetary survival and then explore the message of the mission that's coded within the nervous system and the neuron nucleus. In other words, the mission of DNA is to evolve nervous systems capable of deciphering the mission of DNA.

I hypothesize that the human body is a time capsule. There is a serial unfolding of imprints in the individual's brain that parallels the evolution of the species: the emergence, flowering, and the ultimate disappearance of species from this planet. The first four larval stages of the individual recapitulate the first half (i.e., the early evolutionary sequences) of our species' existence: mastery of the spatial skills to survive on and locomote around this planet.

Humanity reached its metamorphic halfway point with Hiroshima and the Hubble Telescope, which allows us to scientifically investigate the origins of the universe. From now on, we have to consider how to deal with our possible, even likely, extinction. Our species has overrun the material-spatial possibilities of this planet. Those first four circuits, dedicated to hard planetary survival, are a repetitious, primitive drag in comparison with the available potentials of our twenty-billion-cell neural network. The extraordinary levels of dissatisfaction current, especially among the young, are based on an intuitive understanding that gravity-bound meat reality isn't enough anymore.

The purpose of life hasn't changed since Socrates. It's recursive. The purpose of life is to look within and without and to decode the purpose of life. In the 1970s I defined this attempt to decode the purpose of DNA-life with the term *neurologic.* While neurologists studied the biomechanical events that characterize nerve tissue—a subject that posed no more of a philosophic problem than the study of the digestive system—neurologic presumed that the conditioned, educated mind is a tiny, accidentally imprinted part of a total neurological system many million times more complex. Whereas Christian mystics and oriental philosophers relied on platitudes about "God within," neurologic investigated and tuned in to the indisputable chain of creation.

DNA designs and constructs the nervous system. The ego, the mind, and the personality are simply accidental and changeable fragments of the imprinted nervous system. The neurologician attempts to decode the wisdom within using the most accurate description of the external sciences, especially neurology and genetics.

In the 1970s, I believed that the DNA message was about getting off the planet—about migrating, literally, back to our designer. This still strikes me as a good bet. But I've also listened hard to predictions involving escaping biology, changing form, *becoming* information.

One thing for sure, the DNA code has been designing life-forms that evolve from simplicity to complexity for three billion years. We now understand the facts of evolution on this planet, from amoebas to human beings. Since we know that this has been an ongoing process, how do we explain the extraordinary presumption of most scientists that it has somehow stopped with us?

Neurologic perceives every living creature, including every human being, as a potential mutant. Every individual is potentially a highly unique experiment on the part of an evolutionary blueprint. Every human being represents thousands of latent, unique mutant characteristics. Most of the mutations are invisible and detectable only by the most sophisticated biochemical assessments. Many are within the nervous system, morphologically undetectable.

The first goal of a neurologically alert person is to accept the evolutionary perspective: to see the goal of humankind as mutation, to see the human role as student and assistant in the evolutionary process.

This implies the neurological facility to suspend one's larval imprints, to voluntarily and selectively suspend one's personal memory capsules, to transcend conditioned reflexes connected with social role and to become an evolutionary agent, a time traveler: to think and experience like the DNA code.

LEARY THEORY: UP THE EIGHT CIRCUITS

In summary, Leary Theory suggests that:

1) Planet Earth is one of many life-inhabited planets in the local galaxy.

2) Life is routinely seeded (Directed Panspermia) on planets like earth with an unfolding, evolutionary, genetic intelligence by means of amino-acid templates that contain the preprogrammed blueprint of the multibillion-year larval planetary cycle. The planet is a womb, a hatchery. When life has evolved through twelve embryonic stages it might leave the planet and assume self-actualized existence in the galaxy—fabricating what I've called "H.O.M.E.s" (High Orbital Mini-Earths), more commonly referred to as space colonies. The unit of life is the gene pool. In advanced species—social insects, "humants"—the genetic unit is the hive. The key factor in evolution is the formation of new hives by the fusion of self-actualized elite outcastes who migrate from the old hive into new ecological niches.

The nervous system metamorphoses through eight ecological niches:

1. In water
2. On land
3. In artifact shelters (tribal)
4. In cities (insectoid)
5. In hedonistic love nests fabricated by self-actualized bodies
6. In space colonies fabricated by self-controlled brains

7. In self-fabricated DNA hives
8. In quantum gravitational fields

The first four circuits of the nervous system (which have unfolded over the last three billion years) are larval, gravity-bound, and designed for survival in the four niches of the placental planet. These neural circuits mediate adaptation to the four directional attitudes of planetary life:

1. The ventral attitude precedes evolution onto land. Think of an amoeboid creature facing forward to accomplish biosurvival linkage in water.
2. The circuit of crawling onto land involves the attitude of rising up vertically to the appropriate survival posture of dominance-submission, approach-avoidance.
3. The three-dimensional attitude of precise manual-laryngeal manipulation of artifacts and the manufacture of symbols is unique to us language-using humans on this planet. It's facilitated by the dominance of the left cerebral hemisphere.
4. The in-out attitude of sociosexual behavior (sexual impersonation) manages sperm-egg transfer. Here we are involved in the altruistic, collective, cooperative, domesticated roles necessary for the care and protection of the young.

The four postlarval circuits involve an escape from terrestrial, hive, gravity-bound reflexes and make possible transception control of somatic, neural, genetic, and atomic-gravitational realities. What I didn't realize in the 1970s was that we would get to open up and preview living part-time in these postlarval circuits without escaping earth's gravity. We have done this by opening up a new mental space—a new psychosocial ecological niche called cyberspace.

Somatic intelligence is the body as transceptor instrument. The body as one's ecological niche—the hippie generation.

Neurological intelligence is the brain, conscious of its own bioelectric functioning. The brain as one's ecological niche. Brains linked together electronically. The wired-up electronic Web generation.

Genetic intelligence is the transception and synergistic fusion control of RNA signals. DNA as one's ecological niche. The coming ribofunk generation (*ribofunk* is a term used by postcyberpunk SF [science fiction] writer Paul Di Filippo to describe his and others' evolutionary, genetically based SF) of desktop biotech hackers.

The neuroatomic intelligence, transception, and synergistic fusion control of nuclear-particle signals. The nanotech generation.

This is admittedly an optimistic, evolutionary view of human destiny. Indeed, despite the continuingly sorry state of human politics and philosophic mentation, as a scientist I'm convinced that life stacks the cards to win. Physicist Erwin Schrodinger observed that wherever life flourishes, there is the perpetual creation of coherence or information. DNA is pure information. Self-organizing systems, information-forming systems, are a mathematical reciprocal of the entropy process.

John von Neumann and Christian Morgenstern, in *The Theory of Games and Economic Behavior*, get us to envision it in terms of a game of cards. An undirected (random) shuffle produces entropy—because that's the way probability runs. A strategic (stacked) shuffle produces a pattern of order favorable to the shuffler of the cards. Life is the shuffler of the cards, perpetually stacking the energy cards in its own favor, creating negative entropy, pattern, and information.

To win in the game of life, follow the order of the cards. Decode the code. Decipher the meaning of numbers.

SEVERAL EXTRA GRAINS OF SALT

I've learned a lot about chaos since I first transcribed the divine symmetry of DNA wisdom. It still makes a lot of sense to me, but that's part of the problem, isn't it? Life isn't that pat. In this age of chaos, we've all come to understand the limits of determinism.

My DNA wisdom/neurologic theories are both true and untrue—and dependent on your point of view, what time of day it is, if there's a more compelling group of beautiful women at the party, and whether you've mixed wine with cocaine or LSD with DMT. (R. U. Sirius insists that DMT gives you a *bonus* Learyian brain circuit!) Still this abject worship of the DNA code is basically good, healthy, old-fashioned nature worship. After all, the DNA code has enough information to build you an Amazonian rain forest or the Kennedy family.

By the way, never *believe* a word I say. I don't believe in belief. But if you ask the purpose for existence, if there is one other than to make love to *her* better every time, evolving and mutating in harmony with the message of the genetic code is probably a reasonably good guess.

Cyberphenomenology: Who Are You? *Where* Are You?!

> The self comes into being at the moment it has the power to reflect upon itself.
>
> DOUG HOFSTADTER, *GÖDEL, ESCHER, BACH*

FINDING YOUR SELF

In the first section of this book, I am considering (among other things) the nature of the self and of the phenomenological world. Obviously, in order to talk meaningfully about death and dying, we must explore and attempt to come to terms—both scientifically and experientially—with life and living and with the operational processes of the reality we inhabit. In the context of this chapter, I am dealing largely with the *location* of self—the location of individual and generalized consciousness within space and time. In the 1960s and 1970s, young people frequently spoke about their attempts to "find themselves." It pleases me to follow this notion literally. Acquiring intelligence and wisdom about living and dying is a navigational challenge involving both locating and *delocalizing* the self.

Consider the virtual reality of telepresence. You are wearing the transmitter exoskeleton for a robotic teleoperator, your body suspended in a heavily instrumented room. Sensors in the suit you're wearing transmit each of your bodily movements to the distant robot, and force and temperature feedback devices convey to all points on your skin the precise sensations encountered by the remote unit. You're looking into screens that accurately project the images seen by the robot's camera eyes. Through sonic sensors you hear what it hears.

In short, it's as if you are there—wherever the remote unit is—seeing, feeling, doing exactly as it is. Action at a distance, realized.

So there you are, cruising about the world in your own personal simulacrum. The ol' bod is back there in the operator's room. You can travel to distant parts of the world or any world where humans can install robot explorers without leaving home. No bags to pack, no Traveler's Express card to carry. As far as your senses are concerned, the experience is indistinguishable from actually being there. In fact, it's cheaper than piloting your body through real space. The robots are fairly standardized. You can simply rent one when you arrive. Signals to and from the operator's suit can be directed anywhere.

But wait, there is no need for the simulacrum to be far away from the operator's room, either. You walk your simulacrum down the street, which looks familiar. Hey, it's the street that the apartment with your operator's room is on. You walk down the familiar corridor often traveled by your meat machine and open the door to the room where your body hangs in suspension. You peer into the suspension chamber and you see . . . what?

YOU EXIST WHERE YOUR VIEWPOINT IS

Where is the viewpoint, the self? Where are you? Inside the operator's harness, within the meatware of the brain? Or where it seems to be, behind the camera eyes of the simulacrum? My speculation is, in this scenario, the physical body operating the machine would seem alien, as distinct from self as from other artifacts in the world. The sensation of self would be in the simulacrum, where the viewpoint is. You are where you seem to be.

Our model for this experience of self borrows the terminology of computer science, but in fact is found expressed variously throughout cybernetics, biology, and mathematics. We see the human in the world as existing in three parts: (1) one's interior personal world, (2) the external world of artifacts and others, and (3) the interface—the sensory and affective channels through which one perceives and manipulates the external world. The experience of self/consciousness resides at the interface, able to look within or without, toward "imagination" or "reality." Self is a semipermeable boundary.

Symbolically, the situation can be viewed as: ( ), where the pair of parentheses serves as distinction, marking the void to call attention to a difference. Within the distinction is nothing. With our attention on the surrounding context, we see previously unblemished space separated into context and content, inner and outer world.

The courageous reader is encouraged to sample G. Spencer-Brown's *Laws of Form*, from which these protosymbolic ideas are taken. It's a comprehensive and difficult work that gives challenge to cognitive areas that underlie habitual modes of thinking. Brown pronounced the immortal words of understanding phenomena: "Draw a distinction."

Consciousness, self, is symbolized by the boundary generated at the parentheses.

In biology, the analogy is the cell. The cell has an inside, an outside, and a semipermeable membrane that functions as the interface. A computer program has processing, data, and interface mechanisms that acquire the data and produce the results. In the mathematics of distinction, the self—the observer, is the distinction, the boundary between the interior and exterior universes. A change in any of the three components affects the operation of the system.

The Holy Trinity of Catholicism can also be explained as originating from a single distinction. The interior delimited by the parentheses, the space unchanged through the act of creating the distinction, represents the Holy Spirit. It's the most mysterious of the three manifestations of the Christian God, since it is within the distinction, concealed from the outside.

God the Father, the creative force, corresponds to the parenthesis pair itself, the presence of which creates the distinction. God the Son is the space exterior to the parenthesis, the Word sent forth into the world as a consequence of the drawing of the distinction.

But let's return to the simulacrum. The telepresence capabilities of the simulacrum expand the self in space. They widen the interface level by removing it from the traditional boundaries of the body.

Of course, where one chooses to draw the line distinguishing inside from outside, self from other-than-self is formally arbitrary, a matter of operational convenience. In certain mystical states, self expands to fill the universe. In death, phenomenologically speaking, the universe encroaches to diminish self to nothingness. The effect of removing the distinction of self in both instances is identical in the limit. There is no difference and so we might presume that in fact the experiences are equivalent.

The experience of altered boundaries of self have, of course, been expressed and explored prominently by Eastern philosophers. In Western science, Dr. John Lilly, intrepid psychonaut of our age, has engaged in extensive self-experimentation involving sensory isolation tanks (which he invented) and psychotropic drugs. He has produced observations that support our notion of the potential for the decoupling of externally originating sensory impressions from their internal interpretation.

In conditions of sensory isolation, the human input channels usually become filled with novel signals. In common language, people tend to hallucinate. The first tendency among most humans is to interpret these extraordinary signals as objectively real, as having an external cause such as a god or an alien intelligence. It seems more likely that these signals come from within the processing portions of the central nervous system, filling in otherwise empty pathways. Of course, I've earlier conjectured that the central nervous system may have a message for us to decode and that message may, in fact, have been seeded by galactic central. I leave it to you to note the recursive nature of these discussions and, indeed, this book. I also highly recommend the books of Dr. Lilly, specifically *The Deep Self* and *Programming and Metaprogramming in the Human Biocomputer,* for more precise reports on just what occurs when consciousness is disengaged from the usual sensory inputs.

In Western culture, the self is presumed located in the body. Even the crudest of medical evidence further localizes the self within the brain. Sufficient damage to the brain causes coma and, under those conditions, we note the lack of an individual self as we would ordinarily understand it. In contrast, damage to the big toe doesn't have such results (excepting the case of those who have chosen to localize their consciousness in their big toes).

The relativity of the observed, the dependency on viewpoint, is in harmony with the facts of quantum mechanics and observations made by psychedelic explorers. The machinery of mind operates in similar ways, whether processing data arising from the ordinary operation of the senses in perceiving the physical world or operating on internally generated stimuli arising from conditions of sensory deprivation. The same process occurs when the inputs are virtual, computer-generated stimulations of sensory organs or neural pathways.

SELF-REFERENCE AND FEEDBACK

> All Cretans are liars.
>
> EPIMENIDES, A CRETAN

> Don't believe anything I say.
>
> WHAT LEARY THE PRANKSTER ALWAYS SAYS

Watching our "real" body control the simulacrum, through the eyes (cameras) of the machine, we would experience a feedback loop similar to that generated by pointing a video camera into a screen displaying the camera's output. Symbolically, the ability to perceive the extended-in-space interface level would seem to lead to perception of the self-within-the-self—an infinite regress, or hall of mirrors.

The counterintuitive confusion caused in the material realm by the discovery of quantum uncertainty in the early part of the twentieth century has its parallel in the realm of mathematics with the circular causality of cybernetics, dramatically presented in our allegory of the simulacrum. Virtual reality programmer William Bricken puts it this way:

> Self-reference is to cognitive theory as consistency is to mathematical theory: confusion results when either is lacking. . . . Any theory of mind must include within its domain the products of mind, of which theories themselves are a category.

INFINITE PERSONALITY COMPLEX

Rascal "guru" George Gurdjieff and his pupil P. D. Ouspensky held the position that we're all made up of many "selves." A single self controls the person at any given time, and each believes itself to be the only such entity. The impermanent selves vie for control, leading to inconsistency of action as selves with contradictory aims wrestle for control over the helm of being. Gurdjieff believed in the importance of growing a permanent "I" to replace the "false selves" seething within the husk of personality.

More recently, MIT-based computer pioneer Marvin Minsky offered a similar vision. In *Society of Mind,* Minsky convincingly presents the case for the composition of mind as independent interacting pieces of soft machinery whose operation (and, to a lesser extent, interaction) is largely inaccessible to conscious scrutiny.

Circuitous routes of communication—lines of influence—exist between multiple selves. Thus, principles of organization that apply to the interpersonal organization of communicating individuals in an information society might also be applicable toward the *intra*personal organization of selves into a functioning individual.

THE SELF AS INTERACTING FRACTAL SUBSYSTEMS

It would appear then that these systems are fractal, with similar components repeated at each level of scale. I, as a person, am similar to you. Yet the juxtaposition of us and millions of others in a fractally organized system results in the apparent complexity of the system as a whole. The interconnectedness of the world as it appears to humans in certain mystical and pharmacological states comes from a direct appreciation of its fractal nature. It's particularly amusing that nearly every LSD user who is shown visual representations of moving fractals exclaims over his or her astonished recognition: "*That's* what I see."

Think back to the earlier virtual-reality/telerobotic discourse. We might consider asking ourselves the Phillip K. Dickian question, "How do we know we are not operating in a simulacrum now?" Given the fractal nature of reality, what *is* reality? What is really the distinction between the phenomenological world and a simulacrum? We don't know. Lao-Tzu commented on awakening from a dream that he was unsure whether he was Lao-Tzu dreaming he was a butterfly, or a butterfly now dreaming he was Lao-Tzu.

The Mind Contained Within the Brain vs. Mind Unlimited

> That which one believes to be true is true or becomes true at first within limits to be found experimentally. These limits themselves are beliefs to be transcended.
>
> JOHN LILLY, *CENTER OF THE CYCLONE*

EXISTENCE AND DEATH

The identification of self with viewpoint provides some interesting data on the nature of existence and its opposite, which goes under the name of "death" in this culture.

You are alive only where your viewpoint is. What's it like, phenomenologically, to be dead? Well, it's easy to evoke an accurate sensation of this. Where are you, physically, now? Let's presume for the sake of argument that you're not in Algiers. Fine, then *you* are, right now, dead in Algiers. You experience no input or output from there, you affect nothing. People and things there are unaware of you. You don't exist there.

This argument can be extended. You are dead most places in the universe at this moment. Dead in Paris. Dead in New York. (Assuming you don't happen to be reading this in either of those places.) In fact, the only place the self exists is atop a small local pinnacle of space and time.

Of course, this "liveness" has degrees. Timothy Leary is on television right now in Paris. Somebody is reading an R. U. Sirius essay in Algiers. Phone a friend in China. You are alive there—a little bit. Not as much as where your body is, where you see, touch, and perhaps are tasting a delicious chocolate sundae.

The beauty of information/communications technologies is their ability to extend the boundaries of self, to diminish distance and other physical limitations, and permit an individual to reach out nearly undiminished across time and space at the speed of light.

BOUNDARIES OF SELF: INSIDENESS AND OUTSIDENESS

What do we mean when we refer to "your body"? When we speak like this, the question is implicit: Whose body? Who is the operator of these exquisite vehicles of flesh that each of us now locomotes? It may offend some religions, but not reason, to conclude that the notion of self we enjoy is nothing more than an epiphenomenon arising as a side effect of the interaction of mental processing subsystems. To assume anything else is to vanish into a whirlpool regression, a reductio ad absurdum, of dualism: if "self" is something autonomous, apart from the machinery of the brain, it seems that self must have a self.

One recounting of Lilly's experimental observations seems to imply that self—the internal reality—and the rest of the universe are disparate due to their potential for coming decoupled. But the boundary between self and universe is not necessarily fixed.

In fact, the situation is more complex than this. First, what is considered "inside" and "outside" can be transposed at will. The distinction is in one sense real, but the labeling of the items distinguished arbitrary. In *So Long and Thanks for All the Fish,* novelist Douglas Adams plays with the arbitrary labeling of inside and outside through a character who lives in a house that is literally "inside out." The furniture is arranged outside the entrance, and the "interior" of the dwelling contains boundless expanses of space.

But the permutation can be more complex than this. The internal and the external, or truth and falsehood, can combine in ways whose consideration is customarily neglected by traditional Western logicians. Traditionally, any statement can be regarded as either true or false. The missing possibilities are its consideration as true *and* false or neither true nor false.

Dogmatic logicians are aghast as this possibility. Compare this with the brilliant flexible, pluralistic Jain logic of ancient India, based on indeterminacy and a range of seven truth values:

Maybe it is.
Maybe it is not.
Maybe it is and it is not.
Maybe it is indeterminate.
Maybe it is and it is also indeterminate.
Maybe it is not and it is also indeterminate.
Maybe it is and it is not and it is also indeterminate.

The logic we Westerners inherited from the Greeks is extreme, dichotomous, polar. Distinctions are brutal. If you are not on one side, the assumption is that you must be on the other. This is palpably false, and yet look at our political discourse.

To draw crisp borders in the real world is unrealistic. Are you happy? Well, hopefully, but to be coerced to answer yes or no yields an answer with less information than an answer that says, "Yes, 80 percent so" or "Yes, 85 percent of the time."

Berkeley logician Lotfi Zadeh has extended the formal machinery of traditional crisp Aristotelian logic to permit fuzziness, a degree of imprecision the physical world seems to embody. Are you in the room or outside? Well, if you are at that instant walking through the doorway, a real-valued answer tells the inquisitor more than a plain thresholded answer. You might be "almost" within the door.

Zadeh has devised a rigorous system of reasoning with fuzzy linguistic quantifiers like "often," "most," "usually," and "some" to replace the inflexible traditional quantifiers "for every" and "there exists." Of course, you can never use a fuzzy qualifier in a press release, a legal argument, or a political debate . . . yet.

A COLLAPSING OF LEVELS OF FREEDOM

> As above, so below.
>
> FROM THE EMERALD TABLETS OF THE ALCHEMIST HERMES TRISMEGISTICUS

> As inside, so outside.
>
> SLOGAN FOR THE VIRTUAL AGE

German novelist Hermann Hesse wrote beautifully about the experience of personal alienation from the "natural" world. Alienation and rejection are the natural psychological consequences of lack of choice. With only one reality to choose from, one must conform to its rules of operation. Now that computer technology can personalize reality, it becomes less alien and external to us. We become one with it as a consequence of our ability to reach out and transform it, to mold it to conform with our expectations and will with the help of computational machines.

Technology extends the boundary of self; it encloses and makes subjective more of what was objective, or "outside" of us. The area enclosed within the ( ) grows. It is the age of the expanding person.

This engenders a blurring of the material and "spiritual" realms. If by act of will, force of intellection, we can change the appearance of our surroundings (in a self-consistent way, the new reality being coherent in its properties as delivered to our senses), then we gain agency in the realm of spirit. The popular novelist Tom Robbins has said, "Science only gives people what they need. Magic gives people what they want." We agree, but hasten to add that science can give people magic.

Already we see signs of the continued merging of people with their ecosphere/technosphere. Nonlocal interaction is thriving via advanced telecommunications and the Internet. Television extends our sight to distant realms. Where the bounds of "I" stop are determined only by the size of my sphere of influence on the world, and this is increasing continuously for most of us.

Who are you? You are boundless. Where are you? Here, there, and everywhere.

Cyberphenomenology II: What Time Is It? Free Will and the Illusion of Serial Time

> That space is female and time male is a fact (not a fancy or a speculation or a theory or a tradition or a guess) so obvious to a poet that he may forget that it is something that ordinary educated people need to be told.
>
> JAMES KEYS, IN "ONLY TWO CAN PLAY THIS GAME"

The process of locating and delocalizing self involves exploring and expanding our maps and metaphors of time as well as space. Metaphorically, if reality is a movie, a snapshot provides dimensionally incomplete information. Kurt Vonnegut suggests that from a perspective outside of time, humans appear as very long and skinny creatures, distended through time.

The mathematician Jules-Henri Poincairé considered the notion of space the invention of a lunatic for the purpose of describing muscular motions.

By imposing "time zones" on a nation that had formerly let the localities choose their "own" times, the Interstate Railroad Act circa 1880 imposed an illusion upon us all that time is linear.

In *Tertium Organum,* P. D. Ouspensky argues, relative to time, that we would consider it absurd to assume the city one has just left to have vanished from existence and that the city down the road has not yet been created. We presume that all time must exist simultaneously. Otherwise, the present must be seen as an infinitesimally small point surrounded on all sides by a yawning abyss. Under such conditions, the likelihood of another moment would be dubious.

Information/communications technology is doing the wonderful deed of dissolving our addiction to serial time. Jet travel often renders our internal clock out of synch with a region's time. VCRs, and recording technology in general, liberate us from the time clock and continually remind us of the incursion of one time upon another. Email, the Internet, telephone answering machines—all are indicative of a coming "time" when time's flexibility will become as available to postmoderns as it once was to "primitives" who experienced time in entirely different ways.

John Donne, in "An Experiment with Time," explains his precognitive dreams by abandoning serial time. What permitted him to logically dismiss the flow of time as unreasonable is the paradox that the passage of time takes time, hence (by his logic) an infinite regress of times are needed to measure the rate of "first-order time."

Experiences of eidetic (photographic) memory, dreams, and *déjà vu* are aspects of timeless experience, but liberation from serial time is far more sensorially and emotionally encompassing. Instructions for invoking the experience are difficult to transmit, since it's something that takes place deep within the subjective complexity of the individual nervous system.

TIME SPEEDS UP: COMPUTER-HUMAN INTERFACES

Aldous Huxley once claimed that speed (velocity) is the only truly novel drug invented by humans in modern history. While Huxley was referring to velocity of an external, physical type exemplified by the racing of powerful cars, velocity of a more silent, personal kind has similar euphoric effects. In this internal acceleration, electrons carrying the flow of information between artificial and natural circuits (the computer and the human) can jump the inter-entity gap ever faster and more efficiently. The semantic gulf dividing the carbon- and the silicon-based life-forms narrows.

Speed is addictive, and evolutionary.

Individuals who work intimately with computational machinery find they grow quickly accustomed to rapid interactive responses, exulting in the quick succession of events in the cumulative composition or growth of work, in the embodiment of the structure of one's mind in the machine. Being forced to use a slower computer after addiction to rapid-response speed is established is mentally excruciating in the extreme. It seems that there is no return from an accelerated frame of mind.

Many systems evolve unidirectionally in such a manner, from the slower and simpler to the faster and more complex, reflecting the asymmetry of time itself. The directionality of the evolution of the human physical form has carried us irretrievably from unicellular organism to specialized mammal and on toward zero-g space inhabitant. So too has our intellectual level evolved from that of hunter-gatherer to tool user to designer/creator of universal tools (the computer) and metatools (tool-building tools, exemplified by automation in the manufacturing industry).

TIME SPEEDS UP: KNOWLEDGE TRANSMISSION

The brute speed of human-computer interfaces has increased radically in the recent past, however you care to measure it. The trend is continuing.

A mere twenty-five years ago, wood-pulp cards punched with myriads of tiny holes constituted the most widely used computer interface. Of course, a mispunched card had to be replaced—physically, not just electronically, replicated. Clumsy stacks of such cards were dropped, misordered, and lost. The perils of spilled coffee or inattentive clerks were severe. The so-called card decks melted in the rain and smelled when they grew old. The machine was oraclelike, distant from the human supplicant, usually entombed in an inaccessible subterranean air-conditioned glass vault. One had to wait, sometimes for hours, for any indication of the machine's response.

Today, such a baroque mechanism for imparting data to a machine seems almost implausible, a fabrication of hoaxter historians. The computer today is a dialectical partner, an idiosyncratic assistant, usually prompt to serve us.

And in both research labs and cyberpunk garages throughout the nation, innovations are occurring that will make the idea of "typing" to communicate with a machine and looking at output printed on wood-pulp material refined from trees and trucked to vending outlets by gasoline-burning trucks seem as Paleolithic as scratching marks with the graphite core of a sharpened stick to communicate with fellow humans.

TIME SPEEDS UP: THE GAME CHANGES

Speed increases of an order of magnitude change the rules of the game, regardless of what the game is. Automobiles, increasing the speeds of human mobility by close to a factor of ten, revolutionized American culture. We moved around the whole danged country with ease. Air travel is now common, making even lower-middle-class humans world explorers. Space travel makes us all implicitly cosmic citizens. Consider that computer switching speeds have increased by an order of magnitude roughly every three years for the past decade. Off-the-shelf computer workstations have processor chips that run at 500 MHz and provide approximately 2,000 MIPS—2 billion arithmetic operations per second. Their prices continue to drop drastically. Calculations once considered intractable, such as for accurate weather prediction, are now commonplace.

With such accelerated rates of computation, the forces guiding computer programming change radically. When computer processing is cheap and fast, expediency in reducing the time burden of the human in completing a programming task is the most important factor remaining. University courses in programming still focus on teaching techniques to discover the most theoretically efficient algorithm. But the cost evaluations in these calculations discount the ever more relatively precious human time. In certain large-scale problems, the method using detailed analysis of the "computational complexity" of the solution is still appropriate. But in more practical-problem domains, the hack, the expedient solution, is superior. And the human-computer interface is of more crucial importance than the elegance of the computer programs.

Part of the psychological sophistication of a cybernaut rests in her ability to compose effective solutions expediently with ad hoc materials. Cyber adepts can interact with both the material world and the universe of information, cyberspace, in a general-purpose manner. In other words, they employ the hacker's skill of getting maximum use from any system—social or technical—at hand.

The psychological impact of ever increasing human-computer intimacy will be drastic. Today, we award performance—not just thinking about something but actually doing it. Recent developments point toward a relatively immanent direct neural connection between humans and computers that will blur the distinction between thinking and acting to the point where the division can't be recognized. Here we enter the magical realm of psychokinesis.

What will the world be like when "to think is to do"? Already, there are some hints of this through virtual reality, online identities, and role-playing games in cyberspace.

THE NATURE OF THE UNIVERSE: DISCRETE OR CONTINUOUS?

Is the fundamental fabric of the universe we inhabit discrete or continuous in nature? The apparent dichotomy arises in physics, where for decades scientists debated the nature of light. Is light a phenomenon that is continuous, like an ocean wave, or discrete, like shotgun pellets? Evidence exists for both viewpoints: light refracts as do waves, yet it has particulate nature in how it is affected by gravity. Eventually, scientists accepted the paradoxical conclusion that light is somehow *both.*

Heisenberg demonstrated in his "uncertainly principle" that the measurement of the physical world can't be separated from the measurer. It's impossible to exactly measure simultaneously the position and momentum of particles. There is an analogous situation in information theory involving streams of information. To wit: in certain circumstances, one may wish to determine both the probability that a given burst of bits is an *a* and that it's a *b*. The act of measuring the likelihood that it is an *a* obviates the possibility of determining its *b*-ness. Simultaneously checking its *a*-ness and *b*-ness results in a lower accuracy of the determination.

Is the universe fundamentally continuous or discrete? One can only answer "yes."

WHAT'S THE MATTER? INFORMATION

It comes down to this. Matter and energy are frozen clusters of quarks. The smaller the information unit, the more efficient. You needn't chop down a forest of trees to build books. You can put it all on a tiny silicon chip. The universe evolves us toward speed and efficiency.

When stuff, to use a wonderful Alfred North Whitehead phrase, "undergoes the formality of occurring," it's all based on algorithms. Algorithms can be summed up as: if, if, if, if, if, if . . . then. So *if* the sunlight is such, *if* the temperature is such, *if* the water level is such, *if* the meteorological condition is such, and *if* there's enough nitrogen around, *then* all the leaves turn green.

CAVEAT: TRUST IN QUARKS BUT TIE YOUR CAMEL

So matter is information and linear time is an illusion. We suggest, however, that you refrain from dropping a three-hundred-pound barbell on your foot and warn you that the landlord will still show up with outstretched hand on the first of the month. Why the inexorable drag of apparent meat-world reality? How do we get to live according to the real laws of science rather than according to the local ordinances of Prison Earth? This seems to be a tech(nique) problem presented for us to work out. Overcoming these constraints, these limits on our *selves,* is the great alchemical working of cyberculture.

CHAPTER 2

Cybernautics: Modern Alchemy

> We place no reliance
> On Virgin or pigeon;
> Our Method is Science,
> Our Aim is Religion.
>
> ALEISTER CROWLEY, MOTTO FROM THE JOURNAL *EQUINOX*

ALCHEMISTS OF THE MIDDLE AGES DESCRIBED THE construction of magical appliances for viewing future events or speaking to friends distant or dead. Paracelsus described the construction of a mirror of *electrum magicum* with such properties.

Today, modern alchemists have at their command tools of a clarity and power unimagined by their predecessors. Computer screens are magic mirrors, presenting alternative realities at varying degrees of abstraction on command (invocation). Nineteenth-century occult legend Aleister Crowley defines magick—with a *k*—as "the art and science of causing change to occur in conformity with will." To this end, the computer is a latter-day lever of Archimedes with which we can move the world.

The parallels between the culture of the alchemists and that of the cybernaut computer adepts are numerous. Both employ knowledge of an arcanum unknown to the population at large, with secret symbols and words of power. The "secret symbols" comprise the languages of computers and mathematics, and the "words of power" instruct computer operating systems to complete awesome tasks. Knowing the name of something allows one to conjure it into existence. Rites of initiation or apprenticeship are common to both. Action-at-a-distance and manipulation on the astral plane are achieved on command.

Classical Magickal Correspondences

Alchemists of the Middle Ages, and likely before, believed that the cosmos is composed of four elements: earth, air, fire, and water. Although today our periodic table sports more than a hundred chemical elements, the four universal elements still can be identified as the components of any object in the physical world. We also find them useful as basic elements in describing the inner world of humans.

Each of the elements is an archetype, a metaphor, a convenient and appropriate name for a universally identified quality. The four elements are mirrored in the organization of the tarot's four suits: wands, cups, swords, and disks. They also pop up in the four "court cards" of each suit of the tarot inherited from the Egyptians and found ubiquitously in degenerate form in the playing cards known throughout the world. The four also correspond to the four principal tools of the classical practitioner of ceremonial magick.

The wand of the magician represents the phallic male creative force—fire. The cup stands for the female receptive force—associated with water. The sword is the incisive intellect—airy abstraction. Finally, the pentacle (disk) is the grounding in earth—the passive force.

Other foursomes can be found in various magical and religious traditions ranging from Hinduism to the Kabbalah to, of course, the most magical foursome in history—the Beatles (fire: John Lennon; water: Paul McCartney; air: George Harrison; earth: Ringo Starr).

Cybertechnology has its own correspondence with the classical instruments of magic. The mouse or pen of the digitizing tablet is the wand. It controls the fire of the CRT display and harnesses the creative force of the programmer. It's used in all invocations and ritual as a tool of command.

Spinning disk drives are the pentacles, inscribed with complex symbols. They are the earthen tablets set to receive the input of "air," the crackling, dynamic, ethereal intellectual electricity of the processor-chip circuitry that produces computational results. The RAM chips are literally the buffer. They correspond to water, the passive element capable only of receiving impressions and retransmitting, reflecting. (Is the term "buffer pools" a mere accident?)

Iconic visual programming languages can be viewed as a tarot, a pictorial summary of all possibilities activated for divination by juxtaposition and mutual influence. Traditional word-oriented programming languages, FORTRAN, COBOL, PERL and the rest, are a generative form of these universal systems, *grimoires* of the profit-oriented corporate serf-programmers.

The "Akashic records" (i.e., the collection of all universal knowledge) are mirrored by the detailed logs of the activity of operating systems on a microscale. At the macroscopic level, this would be the planetary net knowledge base, the "noosphere" predicted by Teilhard de Chardin, that we are clearly in the process of linking up through the hypertextual network of shared information and knowledge called the Internet/World Wide Web.

Banishing rituals debug programs, and friendly djinn are invoked for compiling searches and other mundane tasks. When the magic circle is broken (segmentation violation), the system collapses. Personal transmutation (the ecstasy of the "ultimate hack") is the veiled goal of both systems. The satori of harmonious human-machine communication resulting in the infinite regress into metalevels of reflection of self is the reward for immaculate conceptualization and execution of ideas.

TOWARD THE HOMUNCULUS

What kind of creatures will we use this modern alchemical power to become in the future? *Homo sapiens sapiens,* the species that has learned how to effectively think about thinking. As we begin to mutate into more effective information-processing entities, our intellectual and physical form is evolving from hunter-gatherer to transmitter-receiver of more abstract forms. At the same time, our machines acquire some of the flexibility and fuzzy logic that characterize human beings (fundamentalists excluded).

One goal of alchemical research is identical with a long-standing dream of artificial intelligence (AI): the production of a homunculus, a small artificial human. (Classical cybernetics has a different dream. It imagines articulating a system so comprehensive that the observer is subsumed.)

The materials of the classical alchemists in this strange pursuit included earth, blood, and sperm. Cybernauts use less olfactory agents. Beyond the issue of humanlike machines and machinelike humans is the future question of whether there will be human-as-machine before there is human-in-machine. We take up this issue again in Chapter 12.

Magick by Numbers

Cybernautics—modern alchemy—invokes the magick of numbers. Cybernetic thinking is antireductionist. General systems theory and its sister cybernetics are studies of holism. They strive to abstract the general principles of process, how things change, from the particular living organism, machine, or mathematical system being observed. Causality is necessarily viewed as circular when the observer is incorporated into the system under consideration.

Classical Newtonian analytic techniques provide good predictive results for deterministic systems of limited complexity, where linear causality is the rule. A falling cannonball is well understood. The calculations involved for anything much more complex than that, however, soon become intractable.

Statistics, through the law of large numbers (which states that the larger the population, the more likely one is to observe values that are close to the predicted average values), can explain portions of the behavior of systems composed of a large number of identically behaving components.

The dominion between these two types of systems is termed by cybernetic theorist Gerry Weinberg as the organized complexity of systems. In these terms, traditional analytic techniques of understanding are confined to organized simplicity, and statistical techniques to unorganized (unstructured) complexity. In this domain, the flexibility and speed of computers serve. Computers are harnessed here not in the brutal solution of huge arrays of equations, but in the flexible and artistic pursuit of modeling and simulation, to locate patterns and make things comprehensible.

THE SCIENCE AND ART OF CYBERNETICS

Classical cybernetics was sired by Norbert Weiner and his physician friend Arturo Rosenbleuth in 1942. Cybernetics abstracts the properties of communication and control in systems from the details of the systems themselves.

The study is transdisciplinary. It matters little to cybernetics whether the system considered is biological, like the human metabolism, or mechanical, or electrical, ad infinitum. The system's activity depends on a flow of information among its elements, and the laws governing control of the behavior of the system don't depend on the traditional dichotomy between living and artificial systems.

As Ashby points out in *What Is New: Introduction to Cybernetics,* "Cybernetics stands in relation to an actual machine—electronic, mechanical, neural, or economic—much as geometry stands to a real object in our terrestrial space." Read that again!

To pursue Ashby's analogy, the modern concept of geometry is no longer dominated by the realm of the possible in physical space. Lines need not meet at a point (Buckminster Fuller). They can be curved (Riemannian geometry of space-time). And they can compose triangles whose angles do not add up to 180 degrees. The geometric configurations that happen to exist in our universe are mere special cases among more diverse possibilities.

Similarly, cybernetics offers organizational principles that underlie all possible machines/systems, including those that happen to exist and those it may be possible to construct.

Chief among these principles is the circular causality of feedback, a notion crucial to the understanding of the complexities of our modern world. Feedback is information about a process used to change that process. One remarkable fact of neurophysiology is that nerve signals don't carry explicitly encoded information. A nerve fiber carries signals to the brain. It is the brain that somehow manufactures the richness of our perceptual experience from these signals. Only by correlating the input signals with the internal state of the perceptual apparatus can sense be made of the signals. Changes of sensation are correlated with motor activity. Here is our circularity again: movements are required for perception, and perception required for movements.

Even seemingly simple muscular acts couldn't be accomplished without feedback. Typing a key at a computer keyboard is a complex orchestration of a dozen muscles tuned and regulated by visual, tactile, and perceptive feedback.

AUTONOMOUS INDIVIDUALS AND SELF-ORGANIZING SYSTEMS

As more and more individuals are liberating themselves from the bondage to authoritarian hierarchical management structures, freeing themselves to interact with the world supported by their wits rather than traditional social rules and relations, I predict that cybernetic principles of organization will emerge within the social system and transform conventional social structure into a fabric whose weave is defined by the sum of interactions of autonomous entities.

As cybernetics pioneer Heinz von Foerster pointed out, cybernetic systems are self-organizing. This implies an active cooperation of the individual components of any population that composes a system. Cybernetics terms this "autopoiesis," from the Greek *auto,* meaning "self," and *poiesis,* meaning "a making." Autopoiesis refers to the central circular quality of all living things and lifelike systems. The principal characteristic of such systems is that their interaction yields systems with the same kind of organization, hence they are "self-making."

For example, an automobile is not an autopoietic system. The processes involved in the operation of the system of a car—acceleration, steering, braking—have nothing to do with the process that generates cars. On the other hand, the product of the operation of the system of a human being is the same as the system itself.

Of central importance to cyber organization is self-reference (i.e., feedback), which leads to fractal, physical (biological, atomic), and intellectual (computer storage and calculation) forms. These principles both reflect and explain the circularity of causality in our world.

TO THE ATOMIC SCALE: THE CYBER-ORGANIZATIONAL PRINCIPLES OF PRIGOGINE

> Our vision of nature is undergoing a radical change toward the multiple, the temporal, and the complex. For a long time the mechanistic view dominated Western science. In this view the world appeared as a vast automaton. We now understand that we live in a pluralistic world.
>
> ILYA PRIGOGINE, I. STENGERS,
> *ORDER OUT OF CHAOS* (1984)

Cyber(netic) organizational principles aren't merely applicable to our emergent technodigital society and to the psychological composition of those living within that system. They pervade the physical fabric of the universe itself.

In 1977, Ilya Prigogine won the Nobel Prize for his work on the thermodynamics of nonequilibrium systems, "dissipative" structures arising out of nonlinear processes. Classical thermodynamics maintained that random (autonomous) local processes such as molecular motion always tend toward a maximum of entropy (disorder). Prigogine showed that in spatially confined neighborhoods, orderly physical assemblages can spontaneously arise. Individual occurrences that engender these spontaneous coherences are called "free agents."

Prigogine's explanations of the phenomenon of convection are considered heretical by traditional science. For instance, we know that hot air rises, but there's no reason why it should; hotter molecules are simply more energetic and faster moving than their cooler cohorts. Prigogine asserts that the coherent emergent behavior of masses of hot air is intelligent and volitional. Hot air rises because it *wants to.* (Some of you, no doubt, will find in this statement an explanation of this book.)

This is analogous to the organizational principles of the cyber society. Although the motion of a single molecule might appear "selfish," aimless with respect to the global organization of its environment, the local interactions of many such individuals produce macroscopic order, in certain circumstances.

THE LAWS OF GRAVITY AND STABILITY REPEALED

Isaac Newton became famous for his establishment of the universal law of gravitation in 1686. A remarkable generalization, it permitted accurate explanation of the motion of the planets and led to the cultural inculcation in European society of a principle of regularity that led to the industrial revolution.

Symbolic of humankind's "triumph" over nature, Newtonian physics made the world appear a safe, predictable place. Given information about the condition of any physical system, physics seemed able to accurately predict its evolution forward or backward in time. The delusion of the pervasive existence of stable and intuitive universal laws in our world gave solace to a species about to lose its one God. It is an ironic comment that this now abandoned illusion of stability is still being hawked in the schools of our nation.

This attitude of regularity persisted through Albert Einstein, who expressed his belief that "God does not play dice with the universe." Today, it is becoming accepted that there are many gods who do indeed play dice with the universe. And many more interesting and elaborate games. In all fields from subatomic physics, to cellular biology, to the raging social mechanisms that balance peace and war, we find what Prigogine calls, "evolution, diversification, and instability."

Developments in the science of thermodynamics—the study of how heat moves—upset the Newtonian applecart. The second law of thermodynamics implies the directionality of time, the world machine running down through an irreversible (and inescapable) loss of energy. Such a universe is not reversible, hence not able to be described statically. Change and disequilibrium are the driving forces.

As we've seen, Prigogine turned conventional doomsday interpretations of thermodynamic results on their heads by showing that coherence and spontaneous order can arise from thermal chaos. His self-organizing, so-called dissipative structures can counterintuitively achieve states of local order. Startling examples include the Zhabotinski reaction, an experiment in which a chemical solution that is far from equilibrium changes color periodically, the molecules changing their chemical identity simultaneously, somehow communicating with one another.

The notion of chaos has a very specific meaning in mathematics and physics today, not at all the same as randomness. A chaotic system is governed by orderly rules, yet its behavior is still unpredictable. Furthermore, changes in the initial state of a complex system, *however small*, lead to arbitrarily large changes after time elapses. Because the initial state is neither precisely measurable nor precisely reproducible, the system is not predictable.

Video feedback is a splendid example of a chaotic system. Point a TV camera into the monitor it's connected to so the camera is rotated 180 degrees with respect to the monitor (i.e., it is upside down). This rotation destroys correlation between successive images. The result is a chaotic system, extremely sensitive to the parameters of camera rotation, lighting, and obstructions placed between the camera and monitor.

LEVELS OF ABSTRACTION AND TOOLS FOR THOUGHT: TOWARD A HIGHER MATHEMATICS

Mathematics itself has been a self-referential, iterative process evolving human thinking away from its initial physical referent and toward increasing levels of abstraction. The first Promethean feat performed in the prehistory of mathematics was the abstraction of the concept of number. Counting systems, placing objects in one-to-one correspondence with other objects such as pebbles or marks, have been with us since probably before we evolved into *Homo sapiens.*

We started the journey of transcendence of the physical realm when we were able to conceive of numbers in the abstract, without the need for continuous reference to an identical quantity of some physical object: cows, apples, or what have you. The notion of "3-ness" as opposed to 3 cows or 3 apples is at a level of abstraction above that of the physical world. It's powerful, because it can be projected into a lower level of abstraction arbitrarily, after computation (arithmetic) has been performed with it in the more abstract realm.

This is the root of "programming," which is an intimation of godhood. One maps one's problem in the abstract and then projects the answer back into the external world.

In other words, numbers exist in the inner world, the world found inside the membrane of self. It's not surprising that mathematics is perhaps the only area of science where the inner realms have achieved complete consensus acceptability, where discussion of the intangibles will never be dismissed as "mystical nonsense."

Rote symbolic manipulations, such as those involved in manual long division, are carried out in the outer world, with marks to represent the numbers. You might say that syntax is an attribute of the outer world, semantics an attribute of the inner.

Of course, these distinctions are relative. When one applies a proof theory to mechanical, i.e., syntactic, verification of the truth of the proposition, one has been able to articulate a means of operating in the outer world with that which was formerly confined to the inner. As knowledge and understanding increase, ever more of the content of the inner world is expressible in languages of the outer.

Abstract mathematics, as Rudy Rucker has noted, has increasingly become a practical technology. This process corresponds to the invocation of heaven into earth prophesied by Crowley. Or as David Bowie put it in his Crowleyan masterwork, *Station to Station,* "A magickal movement from Kether (heaven in the Kabbalah) to Malkuth (earth)." Indeed, the articulation of new mathematical and computational ideas amounts to a continual relative shifting of the boundary between the airy inner and earthy outer worlds.

EXPRESSIBILITY: IRRATIONALS, ZERO, AND INFINITY

The articulation of new abstract mathematical ideas can so challenge the existing assumptions regarding the nature of things that it can provoke a reaction. For example, in the course of his contemplation of the properties of the triangle, Euclid exasperated his contemporaries by the discovery of the so-called irrational number. This entirely new kind of number didn't fit the traditional Pythagorean system based on ratios. One way out of this problem is to permit infinities. Fractions that continue in an infinite regress, a fractal form, permit the precise expression of the so-called irrational numbers.

Understand that until the modern age, the contemplation of infinity was considered absurd by rationalists and heretical by the church. ("Only God can be infinite!") Zero had suffered a similar persecution earlier. It began with that wily number magician Euclid. The acceptance of an infinite number of infinities of different sizes is now commonplace among mathematicians and acid heads.

Higher mathematics continues to get higher.

CHAPTER 3

Language

THERE ARE A FEW TECHNOLOGIES (TECHNIQUES) that are deeply essential to our living processes as a species and as individuals. They are involved in our evolving process of self-definition. This chapter and the two that follow focus on the tools of human evolution and self-definition that I've examined during my life—language, drugs, and psychology.

Today, the thought of humankind is still enslaved by language. Letters follow letters, lined up like little soldiers in proper, sanctioned ranks. Words follow others linearly, the expression being one-dimensional. One is bound by "chains of reasoning" that "lead us" from thought to thought.

Some are so conditioned to the expression of thoughts in words that they confuse linguistic and symbolic mathematical manipulation with thought itself. Nineteenth-century logician George Boole wrote *The Laws of Thought,* a book that defined rational symbolic reasoning processes and provided the operational principles behind nearly all digital computers today, Boolean algebra.

Beware. Words are great vehicles of dogma. "In the beginning was the word." (Later we'll contemplate an alternative view—in the beginning was the drug.)

Many forces are now at work to topple this modern Babel. Hypertext systems like the World Wide Web disrupt and extend the linear structure of text. Television and music videos bring the emotional impact of the rapid juxtaposition of imagery and symbolism into our living rooms. Multimedia communications in virtual environments will be the language of the future, a language including moving pictures, environmental context, the full catalogue of sounds, and eventually touch and taste, as well as the conventional forms of language and text. Unfortunately, as liberating as this is from the traditional textual presentation of information, mostly we're not presently able interact with these images, except by imagination.

Fortunately, many new software and hardware products are rapidly emerging to permit authoring in higher-dimensional media.

Hacking Away at the Word Lines: Modernization of the Definitions of Traditionally Overloaded Terms

We're not big on political correctness, with its insistence on intervening in the funky word models of ordinary people and replacing them with frequently stilted, bureaucratic-sounding word combinations. For instance, Timothy Leary is not "life-expectancy challenged," he's dying (or dead when you are reading this). Still, we've tried gently and noncoercively to offer up new word combinations as a way of breaking habitual thought patterns. Some, like cybernaut (a tripper through the digital world) and SHe/hir (a mix of the masculine and feminine when indicating general humanity), have caught on in some circles. Words are labels that swiftly conjure ideas in the hearer's mind. Words are not distinct packages of meaning, but are tied to clouds of memories and associations. A basic Information Age realization is that these meanings are different for everyone.

In the recent past, this linguistic relativity was less of a factor. As recently as the 1950s in America, there was great cultural uniformity, the marks of tribal organization. Good and bad were still more or less absolute. People seemed to know what was right and wrong. Most people thought, and expressed those thoughts in words, more or less uniformly.

This uniformity has disappeared from under our noses. In the cases of some words, the difference between meanings for different people can be so extreme as to render the word meaningless. For instance, for some 1960s veterans a freak is still a radical, hardcore hippie. In black ghetto culture (and due to the tremendous influence of hip-hop throughout a lot of youth culture generally), a freak today is a promiscuous woman.

To point in all directions is to have no point at all. To be able to think about new ideas, or to think clearly about anything, new languages must be defined. This happens throughout science, the new territories of mathematicians and computer scientists being the most obvious cases. CPU. Floppies. Bitmaps. Jack in. RAM. Trodes. Flatlining.

Creators of other kinds of systems of thought also devise their own languages, those of religion and mysticism. They do so not to be inscrutable, but to be precise. Gurdjieff had a passion for inventing new unpronounceable words to halt the machinelike train of associations that spread from the use of ordinary words.

Word Was in the Beginning

From Plato through Kant to the present, Western society has pretended that for every concept there is an ideal definition, a word or group of words that circumscribes a concept in its totality. The power of the word is traditionally thought to be absolute and objective, meaning the same thing to all speakers of the language.

In *Magick Without Tears,* Aleister Crowley wittily mocks the profusion of arbitrary self-referential symbols that explode from the adoption of language as a system. Any concept A is only defined in terms of concepts B and C, which depend on others, which eventually depend on A once again. To attempt to preserve (or reinstate) meaning in a system devoid of existential contact, mathematics invents formalisms of model theory or semantics and ascribes meaning to yet more complex syntactic manipulations of symbols. Only the illusion of empirical success in their use in communication justifies our continued use of words.

> And then folk wonder how it is that there should be error and misunderstanding in the transmission of thought from one person to another. Rather regard it as a miraculous intervention of providence when even one of even the simplest ideas "gets across."
>
> ALEISTER CROWLEY, *MAGICK WITHOUT TEARS*

The relativity of viewpoint intrinsic to our postmodern culture makes untenable the classical position of the absolute meaning of words. Information theorists assume that something primal and unambiguous is conveyed by the smallest packet of possible information, the bit. But that's only true in a statistical sense, when considering how to maximize data flow through a channel and the like. In practice, bits do not stand alone, but as components in a larger representation that is somehow interpreted by an observer (human or machine), all of it in a context that causes a circularity of meaning to arise once again.

The model in which a proposition's truth is evaluated must always necessarily be bigger than the system in which the proposition is stated. We need a metasystem that forms a basis from which to consider a system. This notion is at the heart of such formal mathematical conundrums as Kurt Gödel's famous incompleteness result. Gödel has shown that in a sufficiently complex system (even ordinary arithmetic is of great enough complexity) there are "truths" that can't be proven true or false except by adoption of a higher-order system. The higher system would, of course, also have this property—it would be incomplete in the same way. Truth is always a relativistic, temporary guess.

There are at least two philosophical positions on how to deal with this brain-squeeze. The dogmatic camp, represented by Bertrand Russell and Alfred North Whitehead in their *Principia Mathematica,* simply forbade the mixing of level with metalevel through a law called type theory. In contrast, the cybernetic approach is to consider semantics as syntax. In other words, we treat any system—including language—as a technology, a useful tool rather than a repository of absolute truth. In doing this, we're also axiomatically merging the observer with the system.

Sophisticated postmodern citizens know that a word doesn't have the same meaning for everyone. At best, it stands for a generalizable concept that we attach differing, specific meanings to. The semantics of a chunk of language can't be understood without including the context of the speakers. The observer(s) must be represented in the system that models what is happening in the conversation. This conforms with the view of classical cybernetics and explains the failure of computer-based natural-language comprehension systems to perform adequately in all but the most trivial of domains.

We have a funny habit of confusing consistency with truth. A system, be it a natural human language, an artificial computer language, or a religion, can be internally coherent and frequently usable without being true.

Language need only be personally coherent to be a useful tool. The sociopolitical studies of Michel Foucault on the politics of language reaffirm in practice the systems theory hypothesis that our thoughts are bounded by the mechanisms through which we express those thoughts. Thus, we can increase personal freedom by expanding our language systems, developing coherent expressions of what previously could not be languaged.

A psychologist named George Kelly developed "The Personal Construct Theory" as an attempt at excavating actual meanings from words and thereby liberating users from those words. In Kelly's system, each individual acts as a personal scientist, constructing frameworks of meaning linking the elements of thought with the ways in which the elements are considered. Interpersonal agreement on meaning can be arrived at through sharing the structure of the frameworks of constructs. The Timothy Leary Software package, *Head Coach,* is based on similar notions of examining the elements of habitual thought by taking apart language and reconstructing new thoughts and new programs.

FROM HUMAN TO MACHINE: MULTIMODAL PARTNERS IN DIALOGUE

The tyranny of languages assembled of words linked by clumsy grammatical conventions today still pervades human culture and restricts thought. As George Orwell, Alfred Korzybski, and Ludwig Wittgenstein have all remarked, any language limits thinking to the bounds of what is expressible in the language.

Our cultural word-based prejudices were also built into languages used to communicate information between humans and computers, even when these languages were chiefly mathematical in nature, expressing numeric and symbolic information in a restricted syntactic form. These built-in restrictions of conventional computer programming languages include linearity: the sequential expression of strings or symbols, one following another as in spoken speech. Thus, we're still restricted to communication that is a priori agreed upon, due to lack of a common substrate from which understanding could be inferred.

One-dimensional written communication is being transcended in a pluralistic media age. TV has long popularized the two-dimensional communication of sound and moving pictures, becoming the primary mode of communication for the second half of the twentieth century. Fortunately, digital multimedia, virtual reality, and hypertext are overthrowing the visually impoverished, antiquated paper metaphors that have enslaved our thoughts throughout the Gutenberg Age.

CHAPTER 4

Drugs

IN THE BEGINNING WAS THE DRUG.

Terence McKenna, among others, has speculated that the evolution from prehuman to human was the result of the synergy of mind-altering plants and the human mind. It seems like a good guess. Apes, foraging for food and never having heard the word *sin,* would undoubtedly have found plants that alter consciousness attractive. Dr. Ron Siegal's book *Intoxication* revealed in the 1980s that getting high occurs throughout the animal kingdom. McKenna points out that small amounts of psilocybin improve visual acuity, which would increase success in hunting, a definite evolutionary advantage for early protohumans. We also know that psychedelic drugs provide insights that are pragmatically useful. Computer programmers and scientists report having the "ah-hah" experience on psychedelics. This is the experience wherein an unthought of solution to a particular problem just pops into one's head out of the blue. We know of at least one computer software designer, who insists on being anonymous, who "channeled" his very successful software program on 500 micrograms of LSD. He wrote everything down on a blackboard with chalk while high on acid. The next day he woke up and began working on the project in accordance with the design he'd "received" on LSD. It worked. He's now a millionaire. We could go on and on contemplating the evolutionary advantages that drugs, including stimulants and painkillers, might have offered prehumans.

The synergetic combination of pain and dope has certainly played an important role in Western civilization, frequently cropping up in tandem with originality in thinking. In addition to Charles Darwin, who tuned in on the web of natural life while taking opiates for his pain, I think of Friedrich Nietzsche, who battled his chronic migraine headaches with so many medicines that Stefan Zweig described the philosopher's tiny room as looking like a pharmacist's shop. I also think of Gurdjieff, whose visions of evolution from mechanistic robotry to cosmic consciousness were all written while suffering pain from war wounds and dosing himself with cocaine and hashish. I think of James Joyce, whose painful eye problems, leading eventually to blindness, were treated with cocaine and who created his now hilarious non-Euclidean "in risible universe" as normal vision faded and "it darkled (tinct! tinct!) all this our funnanimal world." In the repeated cycle of pain-bliss-pain-bliss some especially gifted individuals obtain neurological vistas far beyond the reflex robotry of yokel terrestrial life.

On the Action of Psychedelic Agents

One relevant aspect of the complex action of psychedelic substances such as LSD is their ability to affect the operation of the habitual intellectual "filtering mechanisms" and allow greater detail of lower-level sensory impressions to enter the areas of consciousness usually reserved for more heavily processed signals.

The pulsating, colored geometric patterns typically observed are signals arising in the early stages of the human visual system. Their common frequency, size, and shape are correlated with neural structures in the retina. In one sense, such patterns are always present in the visual machinery. Usually, our attention isn't directed toward visualizing their operation. We are attentive to more processed interpretations of their signals that involve our having classified them in habitual categories. One identifies what is seen with one's mental model of the image without dwelling on the details of the sensory stimulus.

Research into the exact nature of the mechanisms by which psychedelics achieve their effects remains inconclusive, although research—ended during the 1960s by the antidrug inquisition—has finally been allowed to resume in the 1990s. Scientists are looking closely at vasopressin release and the seratonergic system. Since seratonin limits the number of signals firing across nerve cells in the brain, a reduction in seratonin would logically allow for a greater (and possibly overwhelming) flow of signals, leading to glimpses of other interpretations of reality. In any case, the ability of psychedelic drugs to perturb and thus highlight the hierarchical organization of the multiple subsystems and selves within a person is evident.

Through disrupting the ordinary operation of the communicating microselves, the fractal nature of consciousness is revealed to the operator as the cerebral system compensates for the presence of excessive neurotransmitter-like substances in the synapses by rerouting signals though nonhabitual pathways. You get a glimpse at the levels of operation of this system—your self—that are ordinarily below the level available for inspection. Communication between the many complex layers of one's own intellectual composition is made possible.

Contrary to feeling dissatisfied with such a highly mechanistic interpretation of the psychedelic state (so frequently dramatized in mystical terms), we are awed with the view of the realities of the human apparatus that are capable of bringing such experiences into vivid focus.

EACH DRUG HAS SOMETHING TO SAY

We have a problem with molecular monotheism. Even among the most passionate drug enthusiasts, there's this molecular monotheism. Thou shalt have no other drug than psilocybin . . . or whatever.

For more than fifty million years the symbiosis between the vegetable queendom and the mammalian kingdom has been slowly growing. It's no accident that so far something like eighty receptor sites have been discovered in our brain for specific vegetable/plant/chemical messengers. Clearly, we've been programmed for molecular polytheism. As original *High Times*'s publisher Tom Forcade said, "I never met a drug I didn't like." Now, that doesn't mean that different drugs shouldn't be used differently. Or that one shouldn't exercise caution—be more cautious about heroin and methamphetamine (speed) than about marijuana or mescaline, for example. And not every drug is for everybody. Methamphetamine, for instance, is the most toxic of all the popular drugs. It's probably even worse for you than alcohol! It's bad for nearly every organ in your body. On the other hand, a little bit of speed has helped many a college student through exam time. A few thousand individuals are probably doctors or lawyers today who wouldn't have been if not for that moment of communication between their brains and the amphetamine molecules. Back before criminalization, even psychedelic therapists occasionally combined LSD with small amounts of methamphetamine to make the journey more conscious, less sleepy and backbrained.

In the 1960s, I was pious. I came out strongly against heroin and methamphetamine. And I didn't actually experience heroin until the great British psychiatrist R. D. Laing fixed me up. I got a little nauseous and had the experience. It wasn't very interesting to me. But many wonderful writers and artists have produced astounding works under the influence of opiates, from Baudelaire's *Flowers of Evil* to Keith Richard's songwriting and guitar playing on the greatest rock and roll record of all time, *Exiles on Main Street.* Now, as I'm in terrible pain, the opiates offer relief. I've learned to appreciate the high as well. But I also don't take them sometimes and just deal with the pain because I prefer to have sharpness of intellect. But I apologize—not for encouraging informed caution—but for knocking other people's drugs. It's an individual's choice.

The Anti-Evolutionary Message of the Drug War

I've joked in the past about the weirdo oxygen-snorting fish who advanced evolution. But let's be honest. Some fish aren't ready to sniff oxygen. Most of them know who they are. It's been said, for instance, that LSD causes panic among people who have never tried it. Still, if I have prematurely coaxed some fish ashore who were really not prepared for the experience, I now express regret for not refining our invitations with more care.

Unfortunately, it has been very difficult to offer precise and ongoing information and advice about the values and dangers in each and all of the mind-altering drugs. Under the conditions of the war against drugs, which began in the mid-1960s under the Johnson administration in America, the government and mainstream media have endeavored to reduce the level of all discourse to simplicity and outright lies. To this day, drug reportage in daily newspapers is extraordinarily careless. For example, stimulants and psychedelics are referred to as "narcotics." A 1996 article in the *San Francisco Chronicle* said that the disassociative, out-of-body, hallucinatory brain drug ketamine is a relaxant that's similar to Rohypnol (a powerful sedative, the so-called date-rape drug). That's just one example. Suffice it to say that *most* articles about drugs in the mainstream media are *completely* wrong at the level of basic information. Usually the disinfo comes from the Drug Enforcement Agency, where the folk legends that circulate about drugs make the street people in the Haight Ashbury seem like clinical scientists in contrast.

The war against drugs has recently been accelerated by the end of the cold war. Free enterprise "won." Our politicians are suffering withdrawal from severe enemy deprivation. Faced with the seemingly intractable real problems of urban decay, slipping global competitiveness, and a deteriorating educational system, all of it occurring in a time of decreasing government influence, Washington has decided instead to turn its limited powers toward something else that it can't seem to handle very well—the persecution of the twenty-five million Americans who use and traffic in psychoactive drugs.

The elimination of poverty, despair, and the huge profits from drugs would be far more effective than prisons or stepped-up law enforcement could ever be. Decriminalize, regulate, and tax drugs. With one stroke of the pen, President Clinton could erase the violent presence of the domestic drug gangs and the international cartels. But instead, President Groovy keeps the drug war going. We happen to *know* that he knows better. Come on, Bill. It's okay. The voters are wising up. They're showing a disinclination toward drug hysteria (and toward being manipulated by emotional issues in general). Don't let the drug-enforcement, prison-industrial complex push you around. Don't stop thinking about tomorrow. Or yesterday!!! We know about your acid and mescaline trips while at Oxford. The circles are small these days. We all have mutual friends. Don't bogart that joint, my friend. Have my great old friend Jean Houston channel me and we'll talk this one over.

CHAPTER 5

Psychology

IN MANY WAYS, MY *OWN* PRIMARY SELF-DEFINITION has remained linked to that distinctly nineteenth- and twentieth-century technology of self-definition—psychology. My 1950s opposition to the authoritarian, deindividualizing psychology of behavioral control is very poignant to me now as I confront the same authoritarian programs in the medical profession regarding death.

As a 1950s psychological theorist, I suggested that the therapist should not be the one to define optimal psychological health, judge the "patient's" state, and dictate proscriptive and prescriptive decisions. Rather, in *Interpersonal Diagnosis of Personality* and *The Existential Transaction,* I suggested the therapist and the "patient" should work as a team. The therapist would help the patient chart hir own goals and assist hir in hir autonomous decision-making processes. I now see that we need to demand the same transformation from authoritarian to collaborative relationships with our medical professionals.

I was twenty-one when I decided to become a psychologist. It seemed like the most interesting thing to do at the time. Politics was obviously a dreary nonsolution to the problems of human ignorance, fear, and suffering. I had great, though unformulated, ambitions about changing things. I guess we all got more than I bargained for, myself included.

As I studied the practical impact of psychotherapy, I reached a startling conclusion. Exactly one-third of the psychiatrist's patients were getting better, one-third of them were getting worse, and one-third of them were staying the same. You can probably find better results now from "Kenny Kingston's Psychic Hotline." And everybody knows it. But at the time, there was a Woody Allen–style belief in the therapist as the ultimate wisdom guide to existence. I decided that a successful guide would have to have a map of the terrain. So, in 1958, while working at the Kaiser Psychological Research Foundation in Oakland, California, I developed the Interpersonal Diagnosis of Personality, publishing a book by that name. Again, it was all about giving the "patient" the tools SHe needs to explore hir own psychological makeup and game roles. The "patient" could map behavioral reflexes and attempt to change them according to hir own choices regarding where SHe'd like to be on the map. The therapist would be a coach, helping the "patient" to change hirself.

The Interpersonal Diagnosis of Personality (IDP) was very well received and frequently touted as a breakthrough book on psychotherapy. It's still influential in the field of psychology. One of the important breakthroughs in IDP was the notion of self-determination. IDP challenged individuals to examine themselves in practical terms, paying attention to things like the moment-to-moment interpersonal signals they put out, where they chose to place their bodies, and how they chose to respond to specific situations. I suggested moving away from the psychiatric habit of blaming parents and society. I was interested in the acceptance of personal autonomy and responsibility for one's behaviors. This was astonishingly revolutionary at the time.

At that time, I developed the notion of "set and setting" that would later serve as a model for both the psychedelic and the dying experience. "What a person does in any social situation is a function of at least two factors: (1) set, his multilevel personality structure, and (2) setting, the activities and effect of the 'other' person with whom he's interacting." I also offered what I must say was a fairly sophisticated analysis of the implicit sado-masochistic game structures involved in some power relationships. IDP discussed how automatic roles in relationships, however reciprocally damaging, temporarily function to minimize anxiety. People break down when the usual interpersonal signals change. For example, a seemingly positive change in the way a boss treats an underling or the way a guard treats a prisoner can cause extraordinary anxiety. French playwright Jean Genet explored this to great effect in his play *The Maids*. But for American psychology, this was particularly radical stuff.

Further, I added myself to a small but growing chorus of voices favoring group over individual therapy. This notion of teamwork in the art of living and dying has also followed me through my life, right up to my current emphasis on team dying. When we allowed "patients" to react with others in group therapy situations, we enabled them to demonstrate, directly and openly, their repertoire of interpersonal reflexes. Therapeutic groups were miniature societies in which behavioral change could be practiced.

In line with what turned out to be an ongoing attempt to map self-definition and self-location, I was interested in treating psychology in a scientific way. How could we use our brains to do good, to do good well, and do good *measurably* well? I suggested that we develop more flexible, open-ended means for testing these possibilities. For instance, I suggested that we should allow language about psychological change to arise out of the situation rather than imposing existing psychological categories on situations. I proposed that transactions in groups and between "patients" and psychiatrists might better take place in natural settings and conditions, rather than on the psychiatrist's couch, so that we could measure and map behavior realistically.

Most importantly and controversially, I stated that "The subject should be treated as the phenomenological equal of the psychologist in the collaborative research. The patient, after all, is the world's leading authority on his own life. . . . In the sort of research I am endorsing, subject and therapist, collaborators in the joint research, agree on goals and then both work to meet the forecasted standards." This sort of egalitarianism would get me into tremendous trouble later, when it was applied to individual autonomy over brain-change drugs.

Psychology in the Service of War

It's invaluable to understand how the industrial age ideology of factory life and factory death was imposed by the military-industrial complex of the twentieth century.

Human psychology became mainstream during the world wars. For the first time in history, instead of selecting warriors on the basis of how big their shoulders were and how dumb they were, you had to have an intelligent core of bombers, navigators, encryption experts, planners, etc. War became technical. The army used psychological—as well as intelligence—testing to determine "aptitude."

That's how behaviorism—the initial technology (technique) of psychology—got started. The military, of course, always got technologies first. (Now, games and entertainment and the commercial computer industry are at least competitive with the military—one of the many radical changes in the makeup of worldwide power configurations that have occurred over the last couple of decades.)

Before World War I, psychologists operated in respectful collaboration with "subjects." They called it "introspection training," a lovely term that indicates teaching attention, meditation, and self-control. This charming by-product of nineteenth-century romantic individualism was rejected by the behaviorists, who moved in after World War I and sternly defined psychology in terms of objective stimulus-response—scornfully banishing to the shadowy realm of subjectivity any internal, personal response by the "subject."

Right from the start, behaviorism was seen as the special province of the Orwellian manipulators, the secret services, the bureaucrats, the police agencies, and the spies and dirty-tricksters. What a wonderful new toy for the powerful hive-masters: Conditioning! Mind control!

During World War II, the elite of American psychology worked with the Office of Special Services (OSS), which later became the CIA. From their center in Washington, D.C., OSS psychologists developed the science of personality assessment. Candidates for espionage operations were administered batteries of tests and assessed in complex, contrived, simulated psychodramatic situations. The classic example of OSS assessment involved the fake graduation party, which was played out as follows:

After several days of exhausting assessment experiments wherein apparent colleagues (actually planted psychologists) played harassing and confusing roles, the candidates were invited to a party with staff members. Alcoholic drinks were served. The celebration was, of course, part of the assessment. The candidates reaction to the fake camaraderie was actually part of the selection process.

Easy-going, trustful souls were transferred out of the Office of War Information. Distrustful, cagey, paranoid types were immediately screened in as part of the intelligence elite! Thomas Pynchon captures this brilliantly in *Gravity's Rainbow,* ". . . the New Chaps with their little green antennas out for the usable emanations of power, versed in American politics (knowing the difference between the New Dealers of OWI and eastern and moneyed Republicans behind OSS), keeping brain-dossiers on latencies, weaknesses, tea-taking habits, erogenous zones of all, all who might someday be useful." From these wartime roots grew the behaviorist psychology of adjustment.

By 1938, the selection of killer teams involved careful screening for personality traits and aptitudes. From Germany to America and all points between, military psychology became an integral part of the Western war machines.

Diagnosis and treatment of psychological casualties—an entirely new concept in human nature—also developed. Machines break down. Personalities couldn't break down until we defined personality structures in mechanistic terms.

Gravity's Rainbow is truly a spectacular exposé of how manipulative psychologists of the American Skinnerian behaviorist school and the European Pavlovian school were assigned the responsibility, by the military caste, of predicting and controlling human behavior for the purposes of . . . predicting and controlling human behavior.

In 1946 I was offered a well-paying fellowship to graduate school at the University of California at Berkeley. The funding came from the Veterans Administration, an obvious spin-off of the War Department.

During the first week of training, we graduate fellows were assembled. A representative from Washington informed us, with considerable satisfaction, the federal government was getting into psychology "in a big way." The money was going to flow! Great big, fat grants and salaries could be expected!

It happened. In the years following the war, federal support for psychologists in the form of fellowships, salaried posts, and research grants virtually dominated university life. The federal bureaucracy literally paid for and bought American psychology.

What did this money buy? Exactly what the firm wanted—a science of adjustment and control. Branches of psychology that study management of human behavior leaped into prominence: clinical psychology, personality psychology, social psychology.

Leadership in these new fields was assumed by CIA (formerly OSS) functionaries, wise in the ways of government support. The field of personality psychology was covered with the CIA's fingerprints.

Professor Harry Murray, wartime director of the OSS Psychological Project, assembled at his Harvard center the cream of personality researchers. The aim was to investigate and assess normal and successful human beings.

By 1950, most of Murray's staff had fanned out to universities throughout the country in posts of executive power. Donald McKinnon, for example, organized the Institute of Personality Assessment and Research (IPAR) at the University of California at Berkeley.

To IPAR came Air Force officers and successful subjects from many professions to participate in weekend assessments based directly on CIA methods. IPAR was funded by the Ford Foundation, the U.S. government, and several other heavy hitters.

In spite of the prestige, affluence, and power of its staff, IPAR's position in intelligence work was obvious. It had a distinctly subterranean vibe. Its members didn't even show up at psychology conferences. No important papers were published by them. They never had to enter the strenuous competition for funding.

This is not to say that IPAR was idle. It was busy "running" American psychology—monitoring the field, quietly screening new ideas and promising recruits emerging from the graduate ranks, arranging behind-the-scene support for useful research, lining up exchanges of staff with selected foreign departments. IPAR psychologists would pop up in the funniest places. One energetic postdoctoral went along on an Everest climb. Not a bad place for overlooking (surveilling) China.

Another profoundly significant IPAR project attempted to institute a Brave New World psych-tech control. A crew-cut, pink-cheeked, church-going staff member named Harrison Gough designed a personality questionnaire to diagnose "normal" and "superior" persons. The test had scales for "rebelliousness/conformity," antisocial thinking, independence, etc.

Gough received a lot of publicity when he floated the proposal that personality questionnaires be given to every schoolchild in the country in the first grade. It would then be possible to pinpoint at age seven potential troublemakers and future talented specialists. Specialized training and surveillance could then be instituted from the earliest years.

There was no great outcry from liberal psychologists. I found this interesting. Although average psychologists were good-natured, progressive-minded persons, they were amazingly naive and unconcerned about being bought and sold by the federal bureaucracy.

From 1946 to 1960 American psychology was as much a captive of the CIA as Russian psychology was of the KGB. In some ways, American psychiatry was more dangerously coopted, since its ties to reactionary controlling powers were less obvious.

The Behavioral Psychology of Adjustment

The problem with military technology is that wars end. But the winning team's bureaucracies persevere. Germany and Japan rebounded faster than England and France did from World War II because their bureaucracies were destroyed. Anything that destroys bureaucracy enhances evolution.

After World War II, the industries that had been geared up for war production were converted to civilian goods. The managers and tech boys converted the assembly line from tanks to fin-tailed cars. Radar factories went into television manufacturing. America went on the great materialist, consumerist shopping spree that we're still living in the wake of.

Wartime psychological technology was also converted for civilian consumption. Personality assessment techniques were taken over by managerial powers and used to select and train employees. A huge new industry was created to employ clinical psychologists and counselors whose job was to ensure a well-behaved, work-and-consumption oriented, middle-managerial class. This was the psychology of adjustment.

In the 1950s, human personality was seen as a fixed quality that could and should be adjusted to the system.

R. U. WELL ADJUSTED?

Are you well adjusted? Huh? What the fuck does that mean in the highly complex, dissipative, pluralistic yet legalistically authoritarian society of the 1990s? Adjusted to *what?* The center has *not* held. We've come to understand that there is no "normal." That's why the Interpersonal Diagnosis of Personality was formed as a circle. There's no hierarchy. There's no place that you're supposed to end up other than where you *want* to end up.

We exploded the psychology of adjustment in the 1960s. The notion that you make your own way, write your own script in living and dying no longer shocks most Western adults. It's not just the psychedelic movement that gets credit for this tremendous change, it's a whole menagerie of humanist and Human Potential therapists from Abraham Maslow to Eric Berne to R. D. Laing to Jean Houston. The Human

Potential movement and the so-called New Age movement, for all their many faults, have been so promiscuously nonauthoritarian and so generously profligate in disseminating theories and practices for self-exploration that mainline psychology has simply been buried under the avalanche. At the very least, we succeeded in making people so sick of "psychobabble" that we took the behaviorists down with us!

CHAPTER 6

Mutation

. . . Researchers assert that they have cornered for the first time a gene that participates in shaping a specific personality trait.

One version of the so-called D4 dopamine receptor gene, or D4DR, appears frequently in people who report high levels of "novelty seeking," according to two independent studies in the January *Nature Genetics.*

C. Robert Cloninger of Washington University first proposed novelty seeking as a discrete personality trait [one of four, the others being harm avoidance, reward dependence, and persistence]. People scoring high on this characteristic enjoy exploring new environments, are excitable and quick-tempered, and seek out thrilling situations. Those scoring low are reflective, deliberate, and orderly.

Volunteers scoring high in novelty seeking [on personality questionnaires] were much more likely to bear a slightly longer form of the D4DR gene. . . .

SCIENCE NEWS, JANUARY 6, 1996

The Eight-Circuit Model

LEARY THEORY REVOLVES AROUND THE NOTION OF mutation. I believe that evolution is a participatory sport. The Leary Eight-Circuit, Twenty-four-Stage Theory was an attempt to delineate the whole process of evolution and where we fit into it as a species, as individuals, in terms of our generational, cultural imprints, and in terms of the technological stages of our culture.

According to this theory there are eight evolutionary circuits that the human species is designed by DNA to evolve through, four at the "primitive terrestrial" level and four at the "postmodern postterrestrial" level. Within each of the eight circuits, there are three imprint stages. The first stage in each circuit is the receptive stage; this involves passive reception of an imprint at that circuit of evolution. The second stage is integrative. And the third stage involves the exteriorizing process, the transmission of signals at that circuit of evolution.

These three functions are based on the structure of the synapse. The receptor (R) first receives a signal, the nucleus then integrates the signal, and the effector (E) then transmits the signal outward to whatever nerves, muscles, or glands may be appropriate.

Here, briefly is a description of the Eight Circuits and Twenty-four Stages. You should know that SF writer and philosopher Robert Anton Wilson has done a much more lucid job than I of delineating, describing, and defending this model. I suggest you rush out and buy every book the man has ever written, but especially *Cosmic Trigger: The Final Secrets of the Illuminati, The Illuminati Papers,* and *Prometheus Rising.*

It's important to understand that you don't leave the previous circuits behind when you evolve on to the next. You take a basic imprint that will freeze your attitude and aptitude in that stage at the particular time of imprint vulnerability discussed (at least within the "primitive terrestrial circuits"). Imprints can only be changed by shocks that suspend them and allow new ones to be imprinted in their place. This can be done by isolation; illness; years of yogic training; Crowleyan, Gurdjieffian, or Erhardian shock tactics; and consciously guided, high-dose psychedelic drug sessions.

THE FOUR "PRIMITIVE TERRESTRIAL" CIRCUITS

Circuit One: Biosurvival

Stage One. Biosurvival, the passive receptive stage. Evolutionary level: amoeboid intelligence. Individual evolutionary level: infant. Drug that activates this circuit: opiates.

Stage Two. Biosurvival, the integrative stage. Evolutionary level: fish. Individual evolutionary level: infant. Human infants define themselves as self-mobile, fishy individuals pushing toward or away from themselves things they do or do not wish to put in their mouths; they also discover that they can control the external world by crying. Drug: opiates.

Stage Three. Biosurvival, the active transmissive stage. Evolutionary level: oxygen-snorting amphibian crawls onto the earth. Individual evolutionary level: six months old, the child starts to crawl. Drug: opiates.

Circuit Two: Emotional

Stage Four. Emotional, the passive receptive stage. Evolutionary level: small animals—rabbits, rodents, weasels, lawyers. Individual evolutionary level: one year old, the child starts waddling around on two legs and grabbing everything in sight. Drug: alcohol.

Stage Five. Emotional, the integrative stage. Evolutionary level: lions and tigers and bears, oh my . . . and low-level politicians. Individual evolutionary level: terrible one- and two-year-olds, the territorial brat. The child defines hir territory—"my room, my toy, my mommy." Drug: alcohol.

Stage Six. Emotional, the active transmissive stage. Evolutionary level: monkey. Individual evolutionary level: three–four years old, the show-off. The kid starts to master gestures, intuitive charisma, the body language of power or timidity. This is the level that big-shot leaders and dictators have mastered. "I am just a monkey man I hope you are a monkey woman toooooo." Drug: Alcohol.

Circuit Three: Laryngeal/Manipulative

Stage Seven. Laryngeal/Manipulative, the passive receptive stage. Evolutionary level: Paleolithic human. Rote use of symbols. Hunter-gatherer. Individual evolutionary level: four–six years old. The child learns about representing basic realities through language, writing, speaking, signifying. It's all about parroting what you've been told. Up until recent generations, the vast majority of humans never moved beyond this stage. Drug: stimulants.

Stage Eight. Laryngeal/Manipulative, the integrative stage. Evolutionary level: Neolithic. The discovery of fire, the beginnings of toolmaking. Individual evolutionary level: six–eight years old. The child learns how to use words as tools, rearrange them logically, and even invent new combinations. Hey, you're ready to become an editor! Drug: stimulants.

Stage Nine. Laryngeal/Manipulative, the active transmissive stage. Evolutionary level: tribal, division of labor, invention of money as medium of exchange, collaboration. Individual evolutionary level: ten–twelve years old, hangin' wid da homeez. Joining the Scouts, the armed forces. Seeking status by being clever (but *not* nerdily intellectual). Drug: stimulants.

Circuit Four: Sexual Domestication

Stage Ten. Sexual domestication, the passive receptive stage. Evolutionary level: monotheistic, feudal hive-societies based on familial sex roles. Individual evolutionary level: TEENAGER! This is the biggest change since birth, kid. Your body changes and your hormones run amok. You're obsessed with your identity. You're romantic, intense, moody, emotional, cruel, and rebellious, yet growing into your role as an eventually civilized adult. You laugh at adults. Don't ever change *that.* (We have consciously influenced a wonderfully adolescent pop culture that encourages individuals to remain at this stage or to happily skip past the next two dreary stages of socialization, moving directly into the "postmodern, postterrestrial circuits" that start at Stage Thirteen). Drug: *whatever.*

Stage Eleven. Sexual domestication, the integrative stage. Evolutionary level: the family-centered, conformist, bourgeois society. Individual evolutionary level: adult. Fun's over. Settle down. Get a job. Own a home. Conform. Drug: "just say no," Prozac, sedatives, television.

Stage Twelve. Sexual domestication, the active transmissive stage. Evolutionary level: collectivized, bureaucratic socialization. Group safety–oriented totalitarianism. Individual level: senior citizen. Vulnerable, scared, and needing to be cared for. Thankfully, our pop cultural subversion has influenced many of the seniors among us. There are now a substantial minority of hedonist seniors doing their best to enjoy their liberation from wage slavery by relaxing, traveling, taking college courses just because they're interesting, and being as adventurous as possible. Unfortunately, while a substantial number of individuals are redefining the later years of their lives, our society is burrowing ever deeper into this evolutionary stage of fearful, safety fascism. This is, of course, mostly because the wild, postterrestrial, chaotic future represented by the next twelve stages is already rising up—particularly through media and communications technology. And it's scary. Drug: "just say no," Prozac, sedatives, television.

THE FOUR POST-HIVE, POSTMODERN, POST-TERRESTRIAL CYBERCULTURAL CIRCUITS (1960S—TWENTY-FIRST CENTURY)

Circuit Five: Neurosomatic

Stage Thirteen. Neurosomatic, the passive receptive stage. Evolutionary level: hipsters, beatniks, hippies, hedonists, playboys, and playgirls. Individual evolutionary level: slacker. Indolent artist, sensualist, passively hip. You've transcended the guilty domestic circuits and can still giggle at the adults. But you're passive and you can't get your shit together. Drug: marijuana.

Stage Fourteen. Neurosomatic, the integrative stage. Evolutionary level: yogic hipsters, successful hippie artists, happy healers. Individual evolutionary level: hedonistic artist. Practitioners of body arts like yoga, martial arts, dance, playing music, painting. On the downside, you may become something of a self-righteously smug, New Age asshole. Drug: Ecstasy, low-dose psychedelics (psilocybin, LSD, mescaline).

Stage Fifteen. Neurosomatic, the active transmissive stage. Evolutionary level: temporary groupings of self-defining individuals into communes, rock bands, aesthetic brother- and sisterhoods. On the downside, wacky cosmic cults. Individual evolutionary level: you can link that cosmic brain and pleasure-seeking body with another or others similarly inclined. Drug: psychedelics (psilocybin, LSD, mescaline).

Circuit Six: Neuroelectric

Stage Sixteen. Neuroelectric, the passive receptive stage. Evolutionary level: Einsteinian relativity. Electronic media based on quantum reality. Self-indulgent media consumption. Individual evolutionary level: acid head, postmodernist. Reality is all relative to you. Everything solid melts into air. It's all just a dance of electrons. You're jumping jack flash, it's a gas gas gas. But you can't actually *do* anything with this awareness, just groove. Drug: high-dose psychedelics (LSD, psilocybin, etc.).

Stage Seventeen. Neuroelectric, the integrative stage. Evolutionary level: creative use of quantum electric media technologies. The wired-up, digital, DIY home media generation. Individual evolutionary level: hacker, inventor, quantum scientist, media artist. Drug: high-dose psychedelics (LSD, psilocybin, etc.).

Stage Eighteen. Neuroelectric, the active transmissive stage. Evolutionary level: Net communities, global gatherings using media technologies, cyberspace temporary autonomous zones, space colonies. Individual evolutionary level: tantric sex master, psionics (psychic communion) practitioner, global village shaman, Web master, cosmic event organizer. Drug: high-dose psychedelics (LSD, psilocybin, etc.).

It's worth mentioning here that most psychedelic adepts report psychic experiences that aren't so easily dismissed. You know the one where you and an intimate are lying brain to brain, you're tripping out on some particular issue, like whether Timothy Leary and R. U. Sirius work for the CIA, when suddenly you just *know* that your partner is tripping out over the same exact thing? You talk about it and you realize you're both in exactly the same space, sorting out the associations between Leary, Sirius, Tony the Tiger, Bill Clinton, Larry Flynt, Jack Parsons, Pamela Anderson, a half-cat half-dinosaur puking up electrons while skating across your brain on wheels of fire, a tongue made out of Brillo pads and worms, and *your landlord!* And many more of you have had insights into aspects of people's lives on psychedelic drugs that you could never have known, and they turned out to be true. Some of you picked up some great ideas on the acid aether that turned out to be usably worthwhile, from software programs to the notion of starting an irreverent television show for boomers called *Saturday Night Live.* This is all what they call "anecdotal evidence." But the thing is, Mr. Jones, it's an anecdotal world.

Circuit Seven: Neurogenetic

Stage Nineteen. Neurogenetic, the passive receptive stage. Evolutionary level: comprehension of genetics, the Human Genome project, sociobiology, *this theory.* Individual evolutionary level: awareness of influence of genetics on individuation. Tuned in on the DNA code. Drug: high-dose LSD.

Stage Twenty. Neurogenetic, the integrative phase. Evolutionary level: the age of fully realized genetic engineering

(2000–2010). Individual evolutionary level: genetic engineer, pagan scientist operating in harmony with the Gaian web of all life. (Genetics and nature worship are the same thing. Stop fighting!) Drug: high-dose LSD.

Stage Twenty-One. Neurogenetic, the active transmissive stage. Evolutionary level: self-actualized genetic magicians link up to recreate themselves into novel biological, cyborg, and postbiological life-forms (2012?). If we haven't already, we should be swarming beyond the gravitational pull of Prison Earth and becoming galactic citizens. Individual evolutionary level: evolutionary artist, species creator. Advanced forms of technological fusion with other(s). Drug: high-dose LSD.

Circuit Eight: Neuroatomic

Stage Twenty-Two. Neuroatomic, the passive receptive phase. Evolutionary level: self-indulgent use of quantum reality and nanotechnology in postgravitational environment. Individual evolutionary level: highly speculative, probably postbiological life as information patterns. Drug: DMT, high-dose ketamine.

Stage Twenty-Three. Neuroatomic, the integrative phase. Evolutionary level: nuclear fusion combined with gravitational mechanics. The singularity predicted by SF writer Vernor Vinge, beyond which it's impossible for us to comprehend our posthuman selves. We may be migrating toward galactic central! We may have *become* quarks. We may be time traveling. Individual evolutionary level: we are beyond our abilities to comprehend. Drug: DMT, high-dose ketamine, Salvia Divinorum.

Stage Twenty-Four. Neuroatomic, the active transmissive phase. Evolutionary phase: total fusion with all that is. Alternative interpretation—*death.* Drug: DMT, high-dose ketamine, Salvia Divinorum.

ADDENDUM TO THE EIGHT CIRCUITS BY R. U. SIRIUS

Leary developed the eight-circuit model in the mid-1970s while still in prison. During his later years, he didn't talk about it much. I think as he embraced "chaos," he wanted to distance himself from the tidiness of the model. After all, did any of us live perfect, smooth, Circuit-Six, psychedelic, yogic lives? Or did we not, occasionally, get drunk and fall over, trying to be Circuit-Two/Stage-Six show-offs while chasing after Circuit-Four/Stage-Ten femme fatales? But when I think about it, I'm impressed, particularly with how the evolution of technoculture since the 1970s matches his predictions for future evolution.

In a clear gelatin capsule: Circuit Six, the neuroelectric circuit, is already a pop culture phenomenon, otherwise known as cyberculture, wired, the Web, the Net, cyberspace, etc. The notion of living in electricity is with us. More important, it surprised our culture by preceding Circuit Seven, the neurogenetic circuit—biotechnology as a popular phenomenon, which is just slowly coming into its own. When you hear about garage gene hacking, you'll know we've arrived. And who would have guessed that nanotechnology mainman Eric Drexler would come along and begin mapping Circuit Eight, the neuroatomic level, human empowerment on the molecular/atomic level? Ultimately, life may not come in tidy rows of eights and threes, but obviously Leary in his own fuzzy way got it right . . . again.

Mutants Become Agents

We speak frequently of mutants, evolutionary scouts, novelty freaks. It's our intuition that certain human beings from each gene pool, for whatever reason, activate the post-hive, post-modern, postterrestrial neural circuits "prematurely," before the appropriate evolutionary time for those circuits to kick in.

Some individuals are genetically templated to live part of their time in the future. They're alienated from current realities. Sometimes they feel agonizingly out of step with the "normals" around them. Frequently, they are locked away for having visions.

It helps when mutants can recognize themselves. Then, they can view it all with humorous insight. They may view themselves as time travelers. Or they may, like Frank Zappa or Mark Mothersbaugh, look down from on high and offer hysterically funny critiques of larval human behaviors. We find it fun to think of mutants as the real intelligence agents, gathering and broadcasting information for the species.

The word "agent" suggests an unscrupulous bureaucratic scoundrel devoid of creativity, principles, or talent. But the agent is possessed with cunning, which SHe uses in the service of those in power and control. We would like to encourage equivalent cunning among mutational agents.

The *raison d'être* of the agent is the deal. The deal involves the alchemy of linkup, package, and connection. The tools of the agent are persuasion, negotiation, bluff, manipulation, and salesmanship.

The agent caste has existed throughout human history, dating back to the Neolithic period, when artifacts, abstract concepts, symbols, and intertribal barter systems began to replace face-to-face interaction. In feudal times, agents represented the crown or the lord in dealing with serfs, peasants, tenants, and traders. *And,* of course, they dealt with agents of other crowns and lords. Agents were frequently ruthless tax collectors and dishonest traders and would often even betray their masters. Mercenaries. In the democratic period, agents became representatives of governments, classes, unions, guilds, brotherhoods—actors for conspiracies competing for a piece of newly available power.

The history of civilization is the history of agentry. (After all, *agents* arrange for the publication of history books.) During (r)evolutionary periods in history, the mutant becomes an agent for change. The mutant wheels and deals, makes connections, gravitates toward cultural hot points like Hollywood and Silicon Valley, dropping memes (idea viruses) along with names, swapping lies, keeping the inevitable reactionary tide at bay by offering irresistibly sexy, decadent, entertaining rumors of orgiastic lifestyles to be had just beyond the domesticated castle walls if we just keep on keepin' on.

ENTERTAINMENT AS MUTATIONAL SUBVERSION

Recently, cultural conservatives have tried to slow the spread of alienated, mutational insights and attitudes to the democratic masses, the great unwashed, by attacking the entertainment/music industry. People like William Bennett and film critic Michael Medved (in his extraordinarily silly book *Hollywood vs. America)* have put forth the proposition that artists and entertainers should reflect the values of "ordinary" middle-class Americans.

In point of fact, entertainers have always been outcasts whose job is to titillate and shock, and thereby entertain, the rubes, the normals, the talk show–watching housewives. Show business people used to be closely linked with "courtesans." These are the people who traffic in the taboo. Pleasure. Sensuality. Eroticism.

Establishment reality defenders try to discredit the contributions that entertainers, artists, musicians, and courtesans make to the culture. Unfortunately for them, in the media-saturated, rocking and rolling culture of the late twentieth century, the silly, self-indulgent, nonbureaucratic media whores of the entertainment industry have more power to define cultural attitudes than George Will or Gloria Steinem.

It's been a glorious century of subversive messages whispered in the ears of Farmer Brown's sons and Mr. Jones's daughters. From jazz to surrealism, from Picasso to Elvis, from Garbo to Madonna, from the Beatles to Tupac, from William S. Burroughs to Irving Welsh, from Jerry Rubin to Larry Flynt, from the secret messages of glorious sexual liberation spread by the rock and roll radio into the backseat of every car to the blatant anti-authoritarian anarchism that dominates the Internet, it has all gone according to plan!

EGALITARIANISM AND ELITISM

We propose that some members or each gene pool are sired, fired, wired, and inspired to be inclined toward novelty, toward freethinking, toward experimental relationships, toward creative works of great imagination, toward scientific and technological reality hacking. An *elite.*

We also propose that we've pretty much succeeded in making pluralism, freedom of thought, free agentry, ecstatic and transcendent mind experiences, and all the information in the human system democratically available to everybody, as a matter of personal choice on an *egalitarian* basis. (Robert Anton Wilson once commented that it was Aleister Crowley's great genius to democratize decadence. We are only following his footsteps. And we can scarcely take credit for the wonderful job that the music industry has done in this regard.)

There's no contradiction between our enjoying our Circuit-Three/Stage-Nine game of playing (or imagining ourselves playing) these roles as agents of mutational change and democratizing access to drugs and media. In fact, we see that the rise of the Internet and the World Wide Web represents the final victory for countercultural and subcultural mutation. The next generations, raised on the Web as their primary medium, *won't even know what consensus reality is.* They won't even know who the centralized dinosaur political leaders are. The debaters on the *McLaughlin Group* arguing over President Gore's latest strategies will seem as subculturally obscure in five years as *Mondo 2000* did five years ago.

The mutation is a success, Doctor. The culture war is over. WE WON!

part 2

DYING

CHAPTER 7

Dying? Throw a House Party!

He not busy being born is busy dying.

BOB DYLAN

Philosophy is a rehearsal for death.

PLATO

I have known that sense of affectionate solidarity with the people around me and the Universe at large—also the sense of the world's fundamental All-Rightness, in spite of pain, death, and bereavement.

ALDOUS HUXLEY

WHEN I LEARNED THAT I WAS DYING, I WAS THRILLED. I called my dear friend Dick Ram Dass Alpert to share the news. I posted a sign in my home, "THE MOTHER OF ALL PARTIES." All my great friends have come to visit, reflect on the past, help me plan and design my future death, and just plain hang out and have a good time. It's wonderful having everybody come and pay tribute *before* you die, in a spirit of joy and friendship—no morbidity, please.

Instead of treating the last act in your life in terms of fear, weakness, and helplessness, think of it as a triumphant graduation. Friends and family members should treat the situation with openness, rather than avoidance. Celebrate. Discuss. Plan for that final moment.

By all means, stay out of the hospital! Hospitals are vicious, alienating death factories. A tender other cannot sleep with you in a hospital bed. It's not allowed. Your friends can't hang out over a stick of ganja while the nurse gives you something a little stronger to kill the pain. If you can, gather yourself a team of helpmates and experience the graduation at home.

The house party is a wonderful way to deal with your divinity as you approach death. I can't recommend it enough. Divinity is something you have to work at and here you can work on it with other people. Increasing intelligence and awareness is a team sport. Invite people to your house party who share your celestial ambitions. With them, you can write the programs for how you will deanimate. Invite the smartest, most open-minded and well-informed people you know. The amount of information is key. Look within, of course. But look within with other people. Let *them* look within you. Get some navigational advice. Then the story of your soul can be like *Roshomon.* It's a different movie according to each one of your teammates. You get to learn from their vision of your soul and integrate that into your own constant self-redefinition as you choose to.

My Death as Performance Art

When I was informed that I was dying, I realized that some degree of media coverage was inevitable. I decided to define that coverage on my own terms, to die as I lived, in public, being open about my thoughts and actions even when taboo or illegal, so I could use the inevitable attention to challenge society's sense of shame regarding death. I recalled the saddening stories about the death of the great surrealist painter Salvador Dalí, who hid himself away and died miserably. *Vanity*

Fair painted a very grim picture of long, slow decline for this arrogant, imaginative, and brilliant fellow showman. I thought at the time it was a terrible mistake and vowed that I wouldn't repeat that performance if and when my time came.

So I got my team together. My son Zach. The wonderful members of Retina Logic. My eternal partner, Rosemary. All of my great friends. And I determined to celebrate this final act. I would not die in the mechanized factory environment of an impersonal hospital surrounded by strangers.

We started the Timothy Leary Homepage. And we sent out a press release. I announced Designer Dying, the notion that you could playfully plan your death experience and examine the options regarding what to do afterward! Needless to say, the media beat a path to my door.

HOMEPAGE SWEET HOMEPAGE

The Web site was modeled after my belief in home media. Individuals and small groups are now broadcasting from the cozy environs of their homes. This model for media is replacing the big, alienating, downtown office environments that seem to catch otherwise sane humans in the vise grip of player-itis, the tendency to undervalue and underrate the importance of creativity, which is seen as an expendable, replaceable property. Home media, operated by individuals and in-groups, makes for a funkier creative gumbo.

Large corporate entities that have set up "webzines" according to the old model of magazine publishing—expensive office spaces, lots of employees, big spending on the front end—are not surviving in the new environment. We could have warned you. The model for broadcasting on the World Wide Web is a small, flexible, intimate group operating with as little specialization as possible—every team player must be a generalist. Work in the home. Work in the middle of the night if you like. Play in the middle of the day. No urine tests!!! Robert Fripp said it all in the early 1980s when predicting the future of media: "Small Mobile Intelligent Units" was his slogan.

Leary.com (*www.leary.com*) is designed as a tour of my home. People can hang out in the various rooms of the house, checking out my proud possessions (like an original Keith Haring painting) and being informed about the goings-on. They can hang out and chat. During my dying process, they could read updates and reports about the state of my health, my non–medically approved choices of drugs for pain relief, pleasure, or awareness, or they could tune in to the lives of several of my great friends by reading the words of writer and media genius Douglas Rushkoff or the comedian Tom Davis. (Remember Franken and Davis on *Saturday Night Live?* Well, Al Franken's the conservative one and Tom Davis Is a Tall Skinny Genius.)

Aside from being a place where wired-up people can join the party at the Leary home, the Web site is an important repository for potential reincarnation. The electronic storage of books, letters, and other artifacts of existence awaits the day that intelligent systems can build us a new Leary (or a new you), one that can inform, entertain, learn, and perhaps even experience. (More on this in Part Three.)

MY "RASCAL GURU" PR CAMPAIGN FOR DYING AS A GRADUATION PARTY

It was fun, but it wasn't always easy. Nearly every day there was a series of media interviews ranging from the big network newsmagazine shows to "Chuckie's Homepage." We charged the big guys $1,000 and spoke to the small independents for free. Thank goodness every day I had a reason to forego the easy seduction of opioid unconsciousness (I'd save the painkillers till the evening). With whatever discipline I could muster (and the help of nitrous oxide, a marvelous disassociative—it takes you out of your body), I would drag my frequently pain-wracked body out of bed to try to be as sharp as possible in projecting a message of courageous, joyful dying through the media.

Let's be honest. The thoughts were a bit fragmentary. My smooth-talking days were over. But the insights were authentic. I may be so bold as to claim that I occasionally slipped over the boundary from ideas to wisdom. And my dear friend Ralph Metzner told me he never saw anybody do such a fine job of playing the "rascal guru." (As an Irishman, I have never liked being called a guru, but I understand and appreciate where Ralph was coming from.) I received a great deal of love and appreciation from many of my media visitors, and for that I'm eternally grateful.

Of course, seeing yourself projected through the minds of journalists is always an entertaining and informative experience. You've got to learn to laugh and appreciate the extraordinary imaginations of these busy folk. During this campaign, I've been described as a "once-brilliant psychologist," "a sad, spent character," "benevolent," "at one with the cosmos," "the king in his court," and "still adolescent." There's perhaps a bit of truth in each one.

One great thing about being old and "senile"—it liberates you from social games. People *expect* old folks to be crotchety, to break taboo boundaries in social behavior by blurting out honest home-truths, particularly when not suffering fools gladly. In fact, realizing this, the old person often turns sly trickster, taking advantage of the opportunity to have a "second childhood," or in other words another crack at crazy wisdom. All old people have an opportunity to play "rascal guru," in fact. Also, you're forgiven for being fragmentary and forgetful in your thoughts (which means you can get high more frequently!). I must say that, of all my campaigns for thoughtfully challenging taboos, this has been the most genuine, interesting, meaningful, and—correct me if I'm wrong—the best show of my career.

LEARY'S GREATEST HITS: THE DYING YEARS

Here are a few of the things I communicated to journalists about my great House Party for Intelligent Dying.

The following appeared in *The Guardian:*

> How you die is the most important thing you ever do. It's the exit, the final scene of the glorious epic of your life. It's the third act and, you know, everything builds up to the third act.
>
> What does terrorize me is to be an invalid strapped to a bed with ten different tubes coming into me, immobile, a consciousness barely functioning at all, barely able to speak, having my diapers changed. That is worse than dying.
>
> I have no great lust to come back. Well, maybe just for a little while, ten years from now, to meet old friends, have a reunion, and get out by Monday morning.

In *The New York Times:*

> I can't wait for the moment when I'll have the experience of being in my brain without my body being around. I'm working on ways of sending signals, my eyebrows moving, that sort of thing.

◆ ◆ ◆

The no. 1 scientific problem of the twenty-first century will have to do with how to operate the brain. When the heart goes out, boom! The body is dead. But we know that the brain can live on for several minutes more.

The heart stops, but the brain is still there with all those receptor sites still going. When I'm ready to deanimate my body, I want to keep my brain alive for as long as possible.

Nobody has ever answered the question: What food does the brain need to keep going? What food can we give the brain so it's not dependent on the body? With the oxygen on hand, maybe it keeps going for two to five minutes. But theoretically, it could keep working for a very long time.

Even if you've lived your life like a complete slob, you can die with terrific style.

Also, this exchange was recorded in the *Washington Post* by a particularly uptight young reporter. In the article, it came out that a boyhood friend of his who was an acid head and a Pink Floyd fanatic had eventually committed suicide. Can I also be responsible for Roger Water's departure?

"I want you to be relaxed," he says, sucking the nitrous balloon on the way to the cancer treatment. "You're not relaxed."

And neither is he, despite the laughing gas. He erupts when I slow down the car: "Why are you stopping in the road? Why are you stopping!?"

I try again: "When you think back about your work . . ."

"I don't work," he insists.

"You play?"

"You've boxed me in! You've got two categories in your mind: work/play."

"I was thinking about your body of work, the work that you've done."

"What's the work that I've done?"

"You've been a prominent piece of the culture. People have been influenced by what you do."

"Just drive," he orders.

Ahh, to be senile. -)

CHAPTER 8

One Last Taboo for the Road

And in the End, the Drugs You Take Are Equal to the Choices You Make

ONE NIGHT, ON A REASONABLY ENJOYABLE DAY, I posted my daily drug intake on the Timothy Leary Homepage:

Daily Drug Dosage
2 cups of caffeine
13 cigarettes
2 Vicodin
1 glass of white wine
1 highball
1 line of cocaine
12 balloons of nitrous oxide
4 Leary biscuits (marijuana in melted cheese on a Ritz cracker)

Now, if you look at it closely, it's pretty light going. Low-dosage stuff. Still, we hit some nerves when we broadcast it. Big names from the gossip sheets—*tobacco, alcohol, cocaine.*

Even hippies don't approve. My feeling is this: it's up to each and every one of us to self-medicate or not. Our brains and bodies know what they need better than the medical professionals and police authorities do. Especially in dying. What are these drugs going to do—*kill* me? One of the saddest, most sadistic results of the insane War on Drugs in America is that medical doctors underprescribe opioid painkillers to suffering and dying patients. Gosh. You wouldn't want to become a *morphine addict* in the last two pain-wracked weeks of your life, would you?

The issue of self-medication is central to freedom and personal autonomy. Imagine America's drug czar, the seemingly intelligent Barry McCaffrey, announcing federal policy to prevent sick and dying persons from getting medical marijuana. McCaffrey says that there's only anecdotal evidence that smoking grass alleviates the pain, nausea, and other symptoms of AIDS, cancer chemotherapy, glaucoma, and dozens of other dis-eases.

ANECDOTAL EVIDENCE! Say you, or Barry McCaffrey, are suffering great agony. You, or Barry McCaffrey, have tried everything the American Medical Association recommends for your pain, to no avail. I come along and give you, or Barry McCaffrey, something that finally alleviates the agony. You, or Barry McCaffrey, no longer wish you were dead. *That's* anecdotal evidence. It's *your* body. You are not a statistical average awaiting twelve years of FDA testing at an expense of $10 million. You are entitled to control over your body. Even you, Mr. McCaffrey. We humbly suggest that you ask the vice president for his *honest* opinion. And a free sample.

Factory Death in a Factory Culture

But enough of the taboo against being honest about drug intake. We've already successfully put a dent in that one. Let's talk instead about the taboo against conscious, celebratory dying.

The dying person encounters some lame shit in this culture. First, everybody knows you're dying. So what do they do? They come over and talk about Aunt Millie's new car and who won the World Cup. Like you're suddenly an idiot and need to be diverted.

As you get worse, you're probably hospitalized. At the least, you undergo painful and tiresome medical treatments that leave you too exhausted for interpersonal relations. The hospital treats you like a piece of meat. They test, they poke, they give you temporary fixes. Nobody talks to you about your upcoming trip into the unknown. Nobody reviews your quality of life with you. Nobody encourages you to plan from a wide range of death options, whether it be cryonics or gentle euthanasia followed by cremation.

Then, as the great moment of your graduation approaches, they put you in a low-security prison called "critical" or "intensive care." *Now* your friends can't come to see you at all. The warden will only allow card-carrying family members during something called "visiting hours." Listen. I did time in fourteen prisons. I know what "visiting hours" means. It means you don't have autonomy over your body or your interpersonal relations because you're in the joint!

Then, at the tender moment of ascendance, rather than letting you pass on harmoniously into blissful, transcendent illumination, they go into hysterics trying to keep you alive for a few more days of suffering. Imagine approaching a psychedelic experience powerful beyond your imagining, one that might last for eternity—or at the very least *seem* to—and there's a bunch of people around you shouting and somebody pounding on your chest! Talk about punk rock.

Finally, after bumming you out for all eternity, they understandably pass you on to a morbid fellow called an undertaker (your guide to the underworld?), who scams your family for the costly and pointless job of confining your deceased body inside of a tacky, Las Vegas–style wooden box.

FEAR OF DYING

Many wonderful books have been written about the dying process. Elisabeth Kübler-Ross's *Death and Dying* and Stephen Levine's *Healing into Life and Death* come immediately to mind. Let's be honest. Dying with awareness and dignity was already an avant-garde trend before I arrived on the scene. But perhaps I can offer the anti-authoritarian, digital, fun-loving perspective and leave behind a few suggestions as to how to proceed.

Most human beings are taught to face death, like life, as victims—helpless, fearful, resigned. We're schooled and counseled—programmed to act out life scripts based on our worst tendencies toward fear and self-doubt. As we've noted repeatedly in Part One, societies construct systems, bureaucracies, and a common set of "values" that encourage stagnancy and blind conformity. So it's not surprising that when it comes to death—that final glorious moment—most priests, politicians, and physicians encourage DENIAL.

It's certainly not ennobling or empowering to act out the crucial events in one's life with a docile, head-in-the-sand approach. Death is it—the moment we've all been waiting for—the last and singularly most important event we will all have on our resumes. How you die will speak volumes about how you lived.

Throughout history "fear of dying" has been used by priests, police, politicians, and physicians to undermine individualistic thinking, to increase our dependence on authority, and to glorify victimization. As we've discussed, to play the role of good citizen, one takes orders from the designated controllers of society. Those governors demand stability, durability, continuity, and permanence. Staying the course. Showing up on time. Submission. Following the rules. Individual creativity, exploration, and change are rarely encouraged.

Saintly self-sacrifice for the tribe/herd has been the order of the industrial age. Indeed, the very notion of individuals planing their own de- and reincarnations is viewed by priests, professors, medics, hospital administrators, judges, and politicians as insane, immoral, bad for business, and quite possibly illegal.

If your life was dedicated to dutifully serving the reigning religious and political authorities on behalf of the gene pool, then logically your death is the final, crowning sacrifice of your individuality. Monotheists and Marxists would all agree.

And on the other hand, even if your life is filled with happiness and success . . . to what avail? If!?? If awaiting you, implacably, around some future dead-end, some cul-de-sac, are the familiar Old Mr. D. and the Grim Reapers: the coroners, undertakers, morticians, coffin salesmen? What skillful mind programming, what religious-political-medical brainwashing—to program these bleak, grim images and persuade us that we're all victims because we're all gonna *die!* When, where, and how God's agents decree, in fact.

But, hey . . . if you were a good serf, a gentle condominium in God's well-behaved, well-policed, gated community awaits!

THE GENETIC IMPERATIVE: YOU MUST DIE FOR THE TRIBE

In the past, the reflexive genetic duty of top management (priests, politicians, physicians) has been to make individuals feel passive, hopeless, and unimportant in the face of death. Obedience and submission in life and death were rewarded on a consumer-fraud time-payment plan. As a reward for sacrificing their lives in the here-and-now, individuals were promised immortality in a postmortem gated community variously known as Heaven, Paradise, or the Kingdom of the Lord. This was, of course, a sweet deal for the rich and powerful, whose serfs and slaves would willingly postpone their pleasures and never consider rebellion since there were better times ahead after they were dead.

CONTROL OF CONCEPTION IN TRIBAL, FEUDAL, AND INDUSTRIAL CULTURES

We can better understand how the management of the mechanism of dying operates by recalling how humans herds have managed the sexual conception-reproduction reflexes.

- Every kinship group (herd) provides morals, rules, taboos, gestures, words, and ethical prescriptions to control the all-important melodrama of the union of sperm and egg.
- Society manages the horny, heavy-breathing DNA machinery. No incest. You Do Not Covet Your Neighbor's Husband!
- Tribe members are raised to be fanatical about conforming to dress, grooming, dating, courtship, contraception, and abortion rituals in tribal, feudal, and industrial societies.
- Personal innovation in sperm-egg management is sternly condemned and experimenters ostracized.

Industrial democracies vary—from village to village—in the degree of sexual freedom allowed individuals. Totalitarian states like China and Iran provide a less subtle example of this mechanism. The state enforces prudish controls over mating reflexes and governs boy-girl relations, not to even mention boy-boy relationships, girl-girl, dog-and-pony-boy-toy, or whatever other flavor our friends and neighbors are having in San Francisco or Beverly Hills this evening.

Under Mao, "romance" was forbidden because it weakened dedication to the state, i.e., the local gene pool. If teenagers are allowed options, if they select their own mating partners, then they will be more likely to fertilize outside the herd, more likely to insist on directing their own lives, and, worst of all, less likely to rear their offspring with blind loyalty to the gene pool.

HERD SUPPRESSION OF INDIVIDUALITY

The most rigid social-imprinting rituals guard the "dying reflexes." Herd control of "death" responses is taken for granted in almost all societies. In the past, this conservative degradation of singular individuality was an evolutionary necessity. During epochs of species stability, when the new tribal, feudal, and industrial technologies were being mastered and fine-tuned, wisdom was centered in the gene pool and stored in the collective linguistic consciousness, the racial database of the hive. Individual life was short, brutish, aimless. The world was changing so slowly that knowledge could only be embodied in the species. Lacking the technologies for the personal mastery of information transmission and storage, the individual was simply irrelevant—too slow, too small, too brief. (Today, with personalized technology and constant change, the opposite is true. Only individuals and small groups have the flexibility to embody and utilize knowledge. Large institutions are too encumbered.)

Loyalty to the racial collective was the virtue. Creative, premature individuation was anti-evolutionary, a weirdo mutant distraction. Only village idiots would try to commit independent, unauthorized thought.

Feudal and industrial management used the "fear" of death to motivate and control individuals. Today, politicians use the death-dealing military, the police, and prisons to protect the social order. Organized religion and medicine maintain power and wealth by orchestrating and exaggerating the fear of death. The pope, the ayatollah, fundamentalist Protestants, health organizations, and the AMA agree on the basic taboo: confident understanding and self-directed mastery of the dying process shall *not* be allowed to individuals. The very notion that individuals can learn how to operate their own souls and select consumer immortality options is sinful, dangerous to the tribe.

Religions have cleverly turned the rituals of death into solemn, pompous, exaggerated dramas to increase control over the superstitious. Throughout history, priests, mullahs, and rabbis have swarmed around the expiring human like vultures. Death belonged to them.

THE TABOO AGAINST PERSONAL CONTROL OF BIRTH, PHYSICAL MUTATION, AND DEATH

Think of all the hot-button issues that get the church fathers' panties all in a bunch: conception, test-tube fertilization, contraception, out-of-wedlock pregnancy, abortion, euthanasia, suicide, cloning, life extension, out-of-body experiences, occult experimentation, astral-travel scenarios, altered states, death-and-rebirth reports, extraterrestrial speculation, cryonics, cyborgization (i.e., replaceable body parts), sperm banks, egg banks, DNA banks, artificial intelligence, artificial life, and personal speculation about and experimentation with immortality. All things that experiment with the basic issues of birth, embodiment, and death are anathema to the orthodox seed-shepherds, the engineers of the feudal and industrial ages.

Why? Because if the flock doesn't fear death, then the grip of religious and political management is broken. Their power over the gene pool is threatened. And when control loosens over the gene pool, dangerous genetic innovations and mutational visions tend to emerge. Trust me on this.

EVEN OUR FOREFATHERS DID BETTER

Nothing is worse than factory death in a bureaucratic age. We all recall the horror of watching Karen Ann Quinlan, in a coma, forced to stay alive by feeding tubes and breathing machines.

In earlier times, most people died in their own homes. The psychology of denial had not yet formed. People would talk about their souls. Of course, it was all in the context of pious, orthodox, slave religions. There wasn't a great deal of individuality. But at least one had the warmth and humanity of family members. Friends would stop by to say hello. It had more in common with the Leary House Party model for dying than the hospital-prison mode of dying most Westerners experience today.

Frequently, family members would be involved in the bathing and grooming of the dead person's body for the funeral. All the team players were involved in a deep and profound experience that was likely to give them ample opportunity to process their own thoughts and insights regarding death. They didn't just make a quick pass by the casket and then linger self-consciously among the ham and cheese sandwiches. I'm not suggesting, incidentally, that this intimate care of the deceased body be reinstituted, but as an option, it might be worthy of consideration.

All Hail Dr. Jack Kevorkian!

Face it. At this point in human history, we're all terminal. It behooves us to focus some time and energy and courage on regaining personal and group autonomy over the dying process. We have some experience in this department. It was once taboo to talk meaningfully about personal control of sexuality and drugs. From the perspective of someone who came of age in the 1930s, we veterans of the cultural revolutions of the beats and the hippies have seen rapid change in those taboos successfully initiated, even though it's gone slower than we had hoped. Talking about death is the last taboo in our society. And as we've learned, the way to overcome a taboo is pretty straightforward. As the man says, "Just Do It!"

I'm not alone in working on this taboo. Elisabeth Kübler-Ross has done amazing work with conscious dying. My great friend Ram Dass has done the same. And the greatest taboo smasher of all is Jack Kevorkian. He has succeeded, of course, in turning the notion of control over one's own death into a national issue. Imagine the state forcing you to stay alive when you're suffering intensely and have made a considered decision to move on. That's *torture.* Amnesty International should be involved in this issue.

As we've seen, the church hates suicide because that's its turf. It claims full rights to the death property. And the planned suicide of a suffering person takes away that power from the church and gives it over to the person and hir friends and family.

Technology has redefined death. In the past, most deaths were relatively instantaneous. With the evolution of medical technology, scientists have come to view death as a "syndrome." This new language has wonderful implications for those of us who are hopeful of near-future reanimation possibilities. Death, like disease, is now seen more as a cluster of attributes. We've even witnessed the sad spectacle of life after brain death.

The downside of the ability of medical technology to extend life through a long period of dis-ease is, of course, the suffering involved. The upside is that we can now talk meaningfully about Designer Dying, planning the how, where, and when of the final act.

The great hero Jack Kevorkian has taken revolutionary action for the rights of the dying—those experiencing suffering as the result of this extended dying process—to choose their time and method.

Aside from being an angel of mercy, bringing an end to pain, Kevorkian gives people dignity by allowing them choice. He also has made every one of his clients a fellow hero in a struggle against authority and for freedom of choice. I would like to now honor each and every one of them as a freedom fighter.

Kevorkian continues to risk jail and endure public hostility to keep freedom of choice in dying at the top of the headlines and prominent in this culture's social agenda. He's one of the great revolutionaries of the twentieth century.

Kevorkian, in public lectures and interviews, has brought out the historic intrusion of religious beliefs into medical practices. He points out that the first doctors, in ancient Greece, were priests. In the Middle Ages, the priests were doctors. Churches built the hospitals. He speaks of the confusion of religious and medical ethics.

He has also, like me, sought to change the language. In recent times, there's been so much change in language that it's suffered a great deal of ridicule. One of the objections to "political correctness" is that it initiates sometimes distancing, bureaucratic-sounding euphemisms for common usage. But frequently changes in the language are important and significant. These changes are about the way we think about aspects of life and, ultimately, how we experience them. Kevorkian wants to jettison the terms *suicide* and *euthanasia* and substitute the word *patholysis* to mean the elimination of suffering.

We need more activists with the courage of Kevorkian. Before Jack took action, physician-assisted suicide and euthanasia was mostly confined to the world of medical literature. Thousands of articles were written by well-meaning liberal doctors wringing their hands and advocating policy changes. None of them responded directly to the pained cries of the suffering. They waited. They stayed out of trouble. On occasion, medical doctors would more courageously enter the outlaw world of guerrilla patholysis and administer mercy before doctoring the official record books.

Then, in 1990, the brave, freethinking Dr. Kevorkian finally rose up and said to the authorities, "I dare you to stop me." And guess what? For all of his many arrests, not one jury would convict him.

Jack Kevorkian is a man after my own heart, one of the hardcore heretics of the late twentieth century. But I have some problems, I must say, with Jack's style. I even sent him a message about it. I told him that he was treating himself like a victim. He should stop hunching over when arrested. He should get himself a really elegant set of clothes and swagger around. He should stand up and tell everybody, "No more victims, including me." He should cover himself with Hawaiian flowers and have a champagne glass in his hand. But leaving aside these issues of style, Jack Kevorkian has got to be one of the top ten liberators of the 1990s!

HONESTY IS THE BEST POLICY

Finally, the big problem with taboos is that they axiomatically render public discourse dishonest. If you can't say certain things, even though you may think them, even though the scientific evidence may support the taboo viewpoint, this is a loss for the human species. We are here to learn about ourselves, to know ourselves, to ponder the evidence, however uncomfortable it may be to the powerful or, for that matter, the squeamish. Perhaps someday, those of us who are wired, fired, and inspired to challenge this cultural dishonesty will be less necessary. We can move on and deal with other issues. For the moment, we still have a long way to go. I encourage those who have the strength of will and independence of mind to continue to wage the fun campaign in favor of personal autonomy in life and in death.

CHAPTER 9

Design for Approaching Death

Dying with Style

THERE ARE COMMONSENSE, EASY-TO-UNDERSTAND options for dealing planfully, playfully, compassionately, and elegantly with the inevitable final scene. Thinking for ourselves, we can direct and control our final moments of awareness, reaching that level of meaning and understanding variously referred to as illumination, liberation, and enlightenment. If you're prepared, if you're practiced, if you're surrounded by friends and family members who can remind and refresh your awareness of the voyage you're on—then your mind will be free from the constricting games that comprise your personality and the hallucinations and fear that often accompany the dying process. One must simply—with a little help from friends—understand and accept the dying process as one of total liberation. Conversely, failure to accept the responsibility for designing your dying might be the ultimate, irretrievable, final victimization. No matter how you've lived your life, in death you are given a chance that mustn't be denied.

BE PREPARED: EXPERIMENTAL DEATH

One way to expand and extend your options and prepare yourself for dying is to first expand and extend your control over your nervous system, your body, and your consciousness. Therefore, we suggest some methods that might be considered useful in acquiring the experience of "experimental dying," reversible voluntary exploration of the territory between body coma and brain death. The intention here is not merely to gain the death experience but to gain confidence in the experience of going out into the realm of death and then *returning*—for future reference. Experimental dying experiences have been called out-of-body experiences, near-death experiences, and astral travel.

Meditation and hypnosis are useful methods for exploring nonordinary, discorporate, and transcendent states of consciousness. The aim is to temporarily suspend bodily input to the cortical programs, in some cases to attain an out-of-body experience. Gurus and Eastern philosophers have long made the connection between the emptying of the chattering mind that occurs in deep meditation, and death. Buddhists talk about the experience of "no mind." Psychedelic researchers and therapists Stanislav and Christina Grof have also developed a technique, called holotropic breathing, that is known to induce full-blown psychedelic experiences, including psychedelic dying experiences. These techniques are all labor- and time-intensive.

During my experiment in dying, I've found the sensory deprivation tank to be a useful tool in attaining disembodied consciousness, sometimes without drugs, other times amplifying the effects with something as mild as a marijuana cookie. I found that the tank was the perfect place for a life review (one of the most frequently mentioned aspects of reported near-death experiences), and I spent many moments flashing through the movie reels of my life. I have also, on several occasions, broken so free of the Timothy Leary game, and of the corporeal human game, in that tank that it was difficult to reorient upon reentry into physical reality. Interestingly, immersion in virtual reality can have a similar effect.

REPROGRAMMING YOUR DEATH IMPRINT

You can reprogram your approach to dying. To do this, it's necessary to activate the circuits in the brain that mediate that particular dimension of intelligence. Once these circuits are "turned on," it's possible to reimprint or reprogram.

Leary Theory suggests that the most direct way to reprogram an emotional response is to reactivate the emotional experience and replace fear with confident good humor. To reprogram the dying reflexes imprinted by society, it's logical to reenact the spooky, powerful, barbaric dying rituals—then *deflate* them. Simulate a priest, rabbi, or minister and mimic the solemn hypnotic rituals. Recite the prayers for the dying. (No, you don't have to actually go buy robes and do it. Act it out in your mind. Do it in virtual reality. Officiate at your own imaginary funeral.)

Study, educate yourself, trace the origins of your culture's dying rituals. As I hope the previous chapter has shown, the scientific, anthropological examination of taboo phenomena is a fine way to defang fearful superstition.

We see that the rituals intuitively developed by religious groups are designed to induce passive, hypnotic trance states related to "dying." The child growing up in a Catholic culture is deeply imprinted (programmed) by funeral rites. The arrival of the solemn priest to administer extreme unction becomes an access code for the premortem state. Other cultures have different rituals for activating and then controlling (programming) the death circuits of the brain. (Does this discussion of the "dying circuits of the brain" seem too avant-garde or singularly Learyesque? Just consider how every animal species manifests "dying reflexes." Some animals leave the herd to die alone. Others stand with legs apart, stolidly postponing the last moment. Some species eject the dying organism from the social group, etc.)

You can reprogram using the preferred altered-state method (moderate dosages of psychedelic drugs or marijuana, or meditation) to write your own dying script. Words are powerful magick. Many novelists will tell you that when you fictionalize your life experiences, things have a tendency to come true. This is because you're programming yourself to gravitate toward particular types of environments and experiences. You're prepared. The same is true of scripting your own dying process.

Once you've performed a reprogramming ritual or ceremony, store those old, morbid, pious death programs in your "inactive file." (The technique here is your basic visualization, perhaps with the assistance of a moderate dose of your favorite neurotransmitter drug. Visualization isn't just a New Age fad, kids. It's one of the primary techniques of magick and of metaprogramming.) Once you've discarded the old program, format new, happier, healthier programs. I've recently seen myself floating up to an exciting, rowdy, creative heaven where *William S. Burroughs* had replaced the archangel Peter at the gate. Storm the reality studios!

Experimental Dying

THE OUT-OF-BODY EXPERIENCE

One thing we know for sure, death is an out-of-body experience (OBE). Every time you think hard on some subject, you lose consciousness of your body. So in a very loose sense OBEs are a part of our daily life: when we write, think, watch a movie, read a book, surf the Net, etc.

More to our point here, many people have explored intentional, conscious OBEs. This is the experience where you observe your consciousness departing from your body and you view the world from outside of your physical body, sometimes from outside of your physical senses.

Frequently OBEs actually involve being encapsulated in what seems to be an alternative physical form. Practitioners report taking on a variety of shapes, becoming enlarged to cover vast areas or becoming small and flying about at great speed. Sensitivity to vibes or energies is an aspect of the OBE. People who have had this experience report the sense of a soul that separates from the body after death. The sense is one of a self that survives, fully conscious, in an expanded state. Another intimation of death is the frequently reported experience of looking down at the body from which one has just departed. This also occurs even more frequently in near-death experiences (NDEs; see the next chapter).

Spontaneous OBEs tend to happen when one is lying down, particularly during an illness. Specific types of rapid movement occasionally induce spontaneous OBEs. Motorcyclists and airplane pilots seem to be the lucky ones in this regard.

Here are a few steps involved in consciously evoking an OBE, paraphrased from the marvelous *spiritweb.org* site on the World Wide Web:

Getting There

Diet: Avoid heavy foods—e.g., meat or spicy, oily food.

Belief: Imprint a belief system in which out-of-body experiences are acceptable. Remember nonlocality.

Place: Find an uncluttered place, with no electronic devices. It should be a place where you feel safe.

Position: Most people lie flat on their backs. Yogic types may prefer a lotus or half-lotus position. Clear a space so that any jerking motion won't interrupt the experience.

Purpose: Definite your goal. Where do you want to go? No, not the girls' locker room at the local high school. Make it someplace you believe you will be welcome. It's interesting that it's important to map out your trip, where you wish to go, prior to your OBE. Could this be telling us something important about designing our own dying experience?

Drift into a relaxed state: You may want to concentrate on one part of your body at a time. Turn off each body part. Breath deeply and in rhythm. Let your body fall "to sleep" while your mind remains sharp. Focus your energy on your pineal gland or "third eye."

Silence your verbal mind: You can do this by listening to your breath. (There are methods for practicing disconnecting the word game from mindfulness, including reading without verbalizing [hearing the words], typing without verbalizing, dance, and martial arts.)

Leave behind as much as you're able to of your concept of self: Forget your university degrees, racial pride, sexual conquests, political distress, or recent publicity. Try to bring no baggage along.

That's all there is to it. If you're primed for an OBE, you can get there from here. That doesn't guarantee that you *will* get there. But here's what to expect, if you do.

Being There

Be prepared to hear a sound: It will likely be a hum, but it could be something as gentle as rustling leaves or flowing water. If you get an annoying sound, you can attempt to change the pitch to make it less irritating.

Sudden stillness: The onrushing sound and light stop. Don't let yourself be too surprised.

Astral movement: You'll find yourself moving, floating—up, down, around. Don't worry about direction.

Dual awareness: You might feel that you're simultaneously inside and outside your body. This is a transition state. Without trying too hard, shift your attention from your physical body to the astral entity that's moving around. That's where the fun is.

Seeing your physical body: Not everybody wants to dwell on this. Some people will feel fear for the vulnerable body. But looking back on your body offers an opportunity to experience a form of transcendence that is also good preparation for your actual dying experience.

Light!: Be prepared for everything to be shiny and illuminated.

An altered sense of time: Sometimes an OBE seems very brief even though it lasts many minutes or even hours. The opposite is also true—what seems like an extremely long OBE may only take seconds. You are in a different time-space. If you're really lucky, you will see that light is intelligent.

DISASSOCIATIVE DEATH WITH KETAMINE

We have to assume that the best rehearsal for death would involve induction of near-death experiences (NDEs). There's a tremendous body of literature as well as a vast reservoir of individuals who can tell you about this experience firsthand. We'll deal specifically with NDEs in the next chapter.

You can practice the NDE with ketamine. An intramuscular injection of 1–2 cc. will do the trick.

Scientists have recently discovered a tremendous similarity between how ketamine works on brain chemistry and what happens to the brain during NDEs. According to research done by brain researcher Dr. Karl Jansen, conditions that precipitate NDEs release a flood of glutamate, overexciting acting NMDA brain receptors. This can produce brain damage. Ketamine prevents this overexcitation. Apparently, the brain produces it's own ketamine-like brain chemicals that bind to NMDA receptors under near-death conditions and protect the brain cells. Given the similarities between reported ketamine experiences and NDEs, it seems that the altered-state experience is triggered by the action of this substance defending the brain cells from the onrushing glutamate. Also, according to Jansen, "mounting evidence suggests that the reproduction/induction of NDEs by ketamine is not simply an interesting coincidence. Exciting new discoveries include the major binding site for ketamine on brain cells, known as the phencyclidine (PCP) binding site of the NMDA receptor, the importance of NMDA receptors in the cerebral cortex, particularly in the temporal and frontal lobes, and the key role of these sites in cognitive processing, memory, and perception. NMDA receptors play an important role in epilepsy, psychoses, and in producing the cell death that results from a lack of oxygen, a lack of blood, and from epileptic fits (excitotoxicity). This form of brain cell damage can be prevented by administration of ketamine."

Ketamine produces an out-of-body experience that often involves feelings of floating, sometimes through a tunnel. Ego loss is more complete than with the other psychedelics at high-dosage levels. R. U. Sirius had one experience where he spent several moments wondering how all of the information in the universe could be passing through when there was *nobody there* to experience it. Death is very present in the ketamine experience. One senses the thin film between this world and the next. And it's not scary. There tends to be none of the psychological content or the potential for panic with ketamine that one finds when experiencing other forms of psychedelic dying. One truly does not care too much about the world left behind during the ketamine event.

SET AND SETTING AT THE MOMENT OF DYING

In terms of preparing for the actual dying experience itself, the game seems to be exactly the same as preparing for a psychedelic journey. Set and setting are everything. As I've said before, set is the state of mind, how you feel about your soul, whether you're carrying fear with you or whether you're generally filled with positive thoughts and hopes about moving into a new dimension. Setting is where you are. Hopefully, you're not in a hospital bed. Hopefully, you're in a comfortable bedroom, your royal dying chamber, surrounded by the necessary comforts of home—elegant, pleasant furnishings, beautiful and funky works of art, flowers, candlelight, and loving friends.

THE TIBETANS HAD IT RIGHT

The reason our psychedelic research team at Harvard was attracted to *The Tibetan Book of the Dead* was precisely the uncanny knowledge it has about set and setting when entering into the psychedelic dying experience. For Tibetan Buddhists, it is all about your state of consciousness at the great moment. The guide addresses the dying person with the salute "O Nobly Born!" and urges, "Let not the mind be distracted." The guide encourages the departing tripster to get it right, not to become immersed in the projection of thoughts and emotions, fears and desires. As Aldous Huxley said of this book, "The dying are exhorted to go on practicing the art of living even while they're dying. Knowing who in fact one is, being conscious of the universe and impersonal life that lives itself through each of us. That's the art of living and that's what one can help the dying to go on practicing, right to the very end." He added, "The emphasis at the moment of death has to be on the present and the posthuman future, which one must assume to be a reality."

Just think of the distinction between the Tibetans' attitude toward their last exit, wherein the dying person is addressed as "O Nobly Born!" and the Christian attitude, wherein the dying person must ignobly beg forgiveness for his or her sins, or the hospital factory attitude, in which the condemned prisoner must beg for a reduction in the bill.

The Tibetan model, as we understood it during the psychedelic research in which we used the *Book of the Dead* as a guide, is designed to teach the person to direct and control awareness in such a way as to reach that level of understanding variously called liberation, illumination, or enlightenment. It is extraordinary to recall that I had such early practice in the art of dying, experiencing consciousness freed from the cardboard social games that comprise "personality." Indeed. However much we may enjoy our games of fame, glamour, artistry, combat, and the pleasures of the flesh, we psychedelic veterans arrive well prepared—with blown minds—for the experience of "consciousness unbound."

CHAPTER 10

Death Is the Ultimate Trip

As well-spent day brings happy sleep, so life well lived brings happy death..

LEONARDO DA VINCI

Die not, poor death, nor yet canst thou kill me.

JOHN DONNE

First Bardo Instructions:
O (name of voyager)
The time has come for you to seek new levels of reality.
Your ego and the (name) game are about to cease.
You are about to be set face to face with the Clear Light.
You are about to experience it in its reality.
In the ego-free state, wherein all things are like the void and cloudless sky,
And the naked spotless intellect is like a transparent vacuum;
At this moment, know yourself and abide in that state.

TIMOTHY LEARY, RICHARD ALPERT, RALPH METZNER,
THE PSYCHEDELIC EXPERIENCE

LET'S PRESUME THAT DEATH IS THE ULTIMATE TRIP to higher realms of consciousness. As death is universal, the size, scope, and content of the experience is utterly without limits. For every human being, dying will inevitably coincide with the transcendence of verbal word-concept games, perceived space-time dimensions, ego, and personal identity. Intimations of this experience can be obtained in a number of ways. Throughout my life, and in preparation for my death, I've attempted to expand my consciousness in as many of these ways as possible—sensory deprivation, yoga and other forms of exercise, focused meditation, religious and artistic ecstasies, spontaneous understanding, and, most notoriously, through the use of such brain-change chemicals as mescaline, psilocybin, DMT, LSD, ketamine, peyote, and nitrous oxide.

Death, however, is the singular transcendent experience that *every* person will undergo. Dying inevitably unlocks the window of understanding to the outer world of chaos for every single human. It opens each and every mind, liberating each and every nervous system from its ordinary patterns and static structures. As I learned early on during our explorations of the psychedelic experience, how we enter into these basically uncharted realms of higher meaning depends entirely on set and setting. Set is the individual's preparation—his or her personality structure and mood as the final, most important journey begins. Setting is the psychic atmosphere—location, comfort level, social surroundings, the attitudes and feelings of those present as the changes occur—and the cultural environment, how society provides for and allows individuals to go through this process.

One of the attractions of Eastern philosophy is the intelligent examination of death. Those ancient Eastern poets of dying, the Hindus, understood that reality is a dream—a dance of illusion. The Buddhists set down a vision of the universe as a void so complex—as complex as a million trillion galaxies or a million trillion interconnected neurons—that true understanding is unavailable to the rigid, linear, alphanumeric mind.

What Happens When We Die?

Scientists who've studied dying tell us that dying is definitely *not* a slow-lane experience. There's an increase of energy at the moment of death, an increase in vibrational speed. As with neurotransmitter drug experiences, you suddenly shift to a higher frequency. You will, of course, get some chaos, some bleedover or distortion in the transmission process. Fortunately, our neuronauts are ready to tune in to the divine message in chaos.

Remember, you don't die. You just change your vibrational speed. Death is just a different radio frequency.

To try to be a little bit more precise, here's my educated guess: when the body stops functioning, consciousness advances to the nervous system, where it belonged all our lifetime. Consciousness just goes home to the genetic code where it belongs. The genetic code brought us to the planet and she will help us escape from this planet across interstellar infinity to join our family. When consciousness leaves the body, neurological existence within a twenty-billion-cell ecstatic system becomes what we call infinite. When consciousness leaves the nervous system and fuses with the genetic code we receive all life since and before our embodiment.

I predict that dying is a merging with the entire life process. In other words, we become every form of life that has ever lived and will live. We become the DNA code that wrote the entire script. Consciousness returns to the genetic code.

FIELD REPORTS ON DYING

In preparing for death, it behooves us to know what to expect. We are fortunate to have the reports of those frontier scouts who have survived the dying experience. They've provided us with some vital information about what it's like. Here are a few of the aspects of the dying experience.

Any pain that one will suffer comes first. One will instinctively, automatically, biologically struggle to remain corporate. But your body goes limp, your heart stops, and no more air flows in or out. Sight and tactile feeling go. Your hearing is the last thing to go. (Consider the auditory hallucinations and disembodied state of the nitrous oxide experience as possibly indicative of the final moment of embodied life.)

The final moment is not painful. Your identity drifts away but you still exist. Your brain is about to have the most amazing trip ever! For instance, near-death experiences report:

- The perception that one has glimpsed and understood the workings of the universe.
- The literal experience of floating out of the body and being able to look back at the dying scenario.
- Your life flashes before you. You get to review your life, seeing and reexperiencing major events. Sometimes you see an event through another participant's eyes.
- Moving through a tunnel or dark space.
- Meeting others, usually departed loved ones or sacred religious figures.
- Experiencing bliss or terror.
- Seeing a golden, magnetic, and loving light.

EXPERIENCING THE TRANSCENDENTAL BRAIN CIRCUITS IN THE DEATH EXPERIENCE

Everyone has heard of the dying person's visionary flashback perspective. If this retrospective overview is of the observer's own personal life, it would correspond to a Circuit-Five flashback. The subjective memory banks have been rummaged.

If the overview is prehistoric, reincarnate, Paleozoic, and cosmologically thrilling, then the dying process has reached beyond the nervous system into the cellular genetic archives. During high-dose LSD sessions subjects experience dying and report genetic memories and forecasts. LSD has been administered by a few government-approved scientists to dying patients because it seems to resign the patients to their forthcoming demise.

In *The Gates of Consciousness: Beyond Death,* psychedelic researchers Stanislav and Christina Grof report on "death experiences" under the influence of LSD. In their studies, the Grofs and their heroic partners in therapeutic LSD use focused high-dose LSD sessions on the problems of the impermanence of existence: aging, death, and dying.

The Grofs compared the reports from these sessions with the reports from the first studies of near-death experiences conducted by nineteenth-century Swiss geologist Albert Heim. They found the reports virtually identical. The Grofs delineated the most significant experiences for both these groups as: enhanced and accelerated mental activity, unusual clarity of the perception of events and anticipation of their outcomes, and a greatly expanded sense of time. Individuals "acted with lightning speed and accurate reality testing. Typically, this phase was followed by a sudden life review. The culminating experience was one of transcendental peace, with visions of supernatural beauty and the sound of celestial music: . . . Ecstatic feelings of timelessness, weightlessness, serenity, and tranquillity. There were many descriptions of passing through a dark enclosed place referred to as a tunnel, cave/funnel, cylinder, valley, trough, or sewer."

The Grofs further delineate the psychedelic nature of dying as understood by the Tibetans in *The Tibetan Book of the Dead:*

The first part of the Bardo Thödol *[Tibetan Book of the Dead],* called Chihai Bardo, describes the experience of dissolution at the moment of death, when the departed have a blinding vision of the Primary Clear Light of Pure Reality. At this instant they may attain liberation if they can recognize the light and are not deterred or overwhelmed by its . . . intensity. Those whose lack of preparation causes them to lose this opportunity will have a second chance later on, when the Secondary Clear Light dawns upon them. If they don't succeed this time either, they will undergo a complicated sequence of experiences during the following Bardos, when their consciousness becomes progressively estranged from the liberating truth, as they approach another rebirth.

In the Chonyid Bardo, or the "Bardo of the Experiencing of Reality," the departed are confronted with a succession of deities: the Peaceful Deities enveloped in brilliant, colored lights, the Wrathful Deities, the Doorkeeping Deities, the Knowledge-Holding Deities, and the Yoginis of the four Cardinal Points. Simultaneously with the powerful vision of these deities, the departed perceive dull light of various colors, indicating the individual *lokas,* or realms into which they can be born: the realm of the gods *(devaloka),* the realm of the titans *(asuraloka),* the realm of the humans *(manakaloka),* the realm of brute subhuman creatures *(tiryakoloka),* the realm of the hungry ghosts (*pretaloka*) and the realm of hell *(narakoloka)*. Attraction to these lights thwarts spiritual liberation and facilitates rebirth.

According to the Grofs, many schizophrenics report similar experiences of dying. Patients undergoing acute psychotic episodes report dramatic experiences of death and rebirth that frequently involve destruction and recreation of whole worlds. These experiences are also similar to those reported on high doses of LSD, ketamine, and deliriants such as atropine.

ETERNITY: FIFTEEN MINUTES OF BRAIN?

When the body faces a threat to life, alarm signals are flashed throughout the neural network. When these messages indicate that death is imminent, the nervous system shuts off spatial imprints and abandons the outlying sensory and somatic receiving centers. The neural "dropout" begins.

As the dying experience continues, the neural network itself begins to cut out. The energy required to fire signals across synaptic barriers weakens. Peripheral axon and dendrite activity is abandoned. Consciousness retreats to the neuron itself.

At this point, the nervous system operates at Circuit Six, Stage Sixteen. Ecstasy (in its literal meaning of "standing outside") comes to everyone at the moment of dying. The mystical experiences that underlie all religions and spiritual practices have blossomed from the experiences of shamanic, prophetic paleo-neurologicians who experienced these Circuit-Six revelations thanks to epileptic "little deaths," prolonged physical deprivation, traumatic-pathological coma states, plant intoxicants, or because their nervous systems were programmed for experiencing such transcendent states.

The neurological ecstasy of dying lasts no more than

fifteen minutes in clock time. But subjectively it may be experienced as millions of years. The larval imprints, with their conditioned "game" association chronologies, are turned off. Body time is disconnected. The nervous system is free to tune in to its own rhythmic simultaneity, its hundreds of millions of signals per second. The physical explanation of this "external vision of dying" is provided by the Einsteinian-Lorentzian relativity formula: the faster a body moves, the greater the dilation of time. The neurological transformation of this formula substitutes the number of neurons firing per second as the "velocity" factor in the relativity formula.

Let's talk about this some more. Psychedelic adepts reading this book will be able to relate this to their own experiences. In the psychedelic experience, the neuronaut frequently escapes time. We have all found ourselves in timeless moments, in an apparent eternity. And yet, as skin-encapsulated monkey-beings, we ultimately return to the world of social games and physical desires, *even* if we keep dosing. Right?

As we've seen from our discussions of the similarities between near-death experiences, psychedelic experiences, and mystical insights, the dying experience seems to take us into that same timeless eternity. But we no longer need return to form. So while, objectively, the brain may only survive and have the dying experience for three to fifteen minutes, subjectively this trip may last several lifetimes of nearly unbearable lightness, bliss, and revelation. For the psychedelic tripper, finally detached from the inevitable return to overdue bills and game-role attachments, one assumes that there would be no distinction between a subjective experience of several lifetimes—possibly even eternity—and eternity itself. In death, the object of objectivity is extinguished. The subjective experience of eternity *is* eternity!

But let's not be lazy and smug. We're here to express our autonomy and our pleasure in participating in the life process. So why don't we try to answer the question, What food does the brain need to keep it going longer, after physical death? What food can we give the brain so it's not dependent on the body? With the oxygen on hand, maybe it keeps going for three to fifteen minutes. But theoretically, we could extend that trip a very long time. After all, what if every minute of additional objective brain life is several lifetimes of subjective brain bliss?

WE DID THE RIGHT THING

It seems very likely that your final trip will last a subjective eternity, and that how you navigate that final trip will determine whether you have an ecstatic or a hellish experience. It also seems very likely that the final trip is very similar to psychedelic drug experiences. Are *you* experienced?

So you see, Mr. Drug Warrior, it's the experienced drug user who stands the best chance of "going to heaven." SHe who laughs best laughs last. One two three four five six seven, all hip children go to heaven.

part 3

DESIGNER DYING

CHAPTER 11

Picking an Alternative Tech(nique) from the Evolutionary Menu

We recognize that the dying process, which for millennia has been blanketed by taboo and primitive superstition, has suddenly become accessible to human intelligence. It's possible to consider technological alternatives to irreversible death.

Here we experience the sudden insight that we need not go "quietly" and passively into that dark night or the neon-lit, Muzak-enhanced Disney-heaven of the Jesus Gang. We predict that the concept of involuntary, irreversible metabolic coma known as "death" is about to become an outmoded, antiquated superstition.

We understand that there are already a few active, creative alternatives to going belly-up clutching the company logo of the Christian cross, Blue Cross, or the Red Crescent or the dread victim-eligibility cards of the Veterans Administration. Recognizing this is the start in challenging the grim authority of irreversible death. Once we comprehend that "death" is a problem of knowledge—information processing—solutions can emerge.

This chapter briefly identifies a few of the options. We'll explore my favorites in greater detail in the rest of Part Three.

The Postbiological Options of the Information Species

A fascinating set of gourmet consumer choices regarding death have suddenly appeared on the pop-up menu of the Evolutionary Cafe. It seems plausible that individuals in information societies can script, produce, and direct their own hibernation/reanimations.

An intelligent option is to try to keep our knowledge-processing capacities around as long as possible. In bodily form. In neural norm. In DNA form. In magnetic-digital storage. In molecular form, through the atom-stacking of nanotechnology in tomorrow's computers. In cryogenic form. In the form of stored data, legend, myth. In the form of offspring who are cybernetically trained to use postbiological intelligence. In the form of postbiological gene pools, info pools, and advanced viral forms resident in world computer networks and cyberspace matrices of the sort described in the "sprawl novels" of William Gibson.

SOUL DEANIMATION

Before further delineating hibernation and postbiological options, let's review some methods for managing the biological aspects of soul deanimation. The techniques in this category do not assist in attaining personal immortality per se, but are important in that they're indicative of increased options in autonomous control over the dying process. We've touched on these already in Part Two. These include:

Voluntary Deanimation (Self-deliverance): This procedure is called "suicide," i.e., "self-murder," by officials who wish to control the dying process. Until recently, self-induced death has been considered a cowardly or insane attempt to interfere with the natural order. Those who wished to manage and direct their own dying were condemned by law and custom.

Pagan, Humanist Natural Deanimation: In a pagan or nature-attuned tribal culture, there is a commonsense genetic wisdom implied in the passive acceptance of one's termination. The brain continually monitors the vital functions of the body and as the body starts failing, terminal programs take over. The brain quietly shuts down the body and during the few minutes between body death and neurological death, the brain's two hundred billion neurons probably enjoy an astonishing "timeless" review of all and everything.

Mechanical medicine interferes with this natural deanimation. Tubes and machines are now used to keep patients alive long after the cessation of consciousness. A stroke victim who twenty years ago might have died in an hour can now be revived, only to spend years in a machine-supported coma.

Most people are shocked and outraged by mechanical medical methods that strip dignity and human consciousness from the terminal coma patient. Even the American Medical Association has supported the right of the family to remove medical treatment from terminally ill comatose patients.

Then there is the problem of intractable, agonizing pain suffered by patients terminally ill from "artificial" diseases, like cancer, caused by industrial pollution. The brain housed in the body of a person living in the industrial, low-rent, tacky culture of the late twentieth century is not programmed to handle these new diseases. The brain is capable of producing endorphin painkillers naturally, but not in adequate supply to handle the pains of industrial dying (or, in many cases, industrial living). The brain is beautifully geared to slowly, gracefully turn out the lights for humans as it does for other animals. Our sisters and brothers, the other pack animals like wolves, dogs, and cats, manage to die in dignity without screaming to veterinarians for sedation or priests for "extreme unction." But the hospital-factory environment is a very strange terrain for any normal two-hundred-billion-neuron brain. So, hospitalized patients whose brains are imprinted to perform as factory units when terminally ill and in great pain passionately beg to be put out of their hopeless misery.

Fundamentalist religious groups and neofeudal officials oppose any "pro-choice" initiative that allows individuals to manage their own lives. This naturally includes "euthanasia." But the movement for freedom to naturally deanimate has grown to embrace a majority of the voting American public. The (r)evolutionary shock tactics of Jack Kevorkian and others are speeding us toward the inevitable. It seems likely that by the end of the next decade, ceremonial, dignified celebration of one's own dying will be considered a basic human ritual.

Technological Preservations

We are beginning to understand ourselves as information processes. We are also in the middle of an astounding revolution in information storage and exchange. Finally, we're at the raw beginnings of the technology of manipulating matter as information. All of this indicates to me that information technology is a technology of self-preservation. Some forms of technological self-preservation involve the possibility of return in physical form. Others involve only the digital preservation of an individual's unique information patterns for the future edification and enjoyment of others. We will look briefly at both forms.

PREMORTEM HIBERNATION

The graceful, planned process of dying takes on a different meaning when the person does not "die" but slides into cryonic or brain-bank hibernation. This option is called "premortem suspension." It has been ruled legal in California in a case brought by the ALCOR Foundation of Riverside, California.

SOMATIC/NEURAL/GENETIC PRESERVATION

Techniques in this class do not ensure continuous operation of consciousness. They produce reversible metabolic coma. They are alternatives for preserving the structure of tissues until a time of more advanced medical knowledge. These include:

Cryogenics, or vacuum-pack "pickling": Why let one's body and brain rot when that seems to imply no possibility at all for your future? Why let the carefully arranged tangle of dendritic growths in your nervous system that store all of your memories get eaten by fungus? Perpetual preservation of your tissues is available today at moderate cost.

Cryonic preservation of neural tissue or DNA: Those not particularly attached to their bodies can opt for preservation of the essentials: their brains and the instructional codes capable of regrouping something genetically identical to their present biomachinery.

System upgrades, cyborgization for life extension: Is there any need to experience metabolic coma? Techniques are now emerging to permit a much more vivid guarantee of personal persistence, a smooth metamorphic transformation into a different form of substrate on which the computer program of consciousness runs.

Cellular/DNA repair: Nanotechnology is the science and engineering of mechanical and electronic systems built to atomic specifications. One forecast ability of nanotechnology is its potential to produce self-replicating nanomachines that live within individual biological cells. These artificial enzymes will effect cellular repair as damage occurs from mechanical causes, radiation, or other aging effects. Repair of DNA ensures genetic stability.

Cloning: Biologically based replication of genetically identical personal copies of yourself, at any time desired, will be available in the very near future. Sex is fun, but sexual reproduction is biologically inefficient; it is suited mainly for inducing genetic variation in species that still advance through the accidents in random combination. The idea is to reserve sex as a means of communication and to reproduce asexually!

CYBERNETIC METHODS FOR ATTAINING IMMORTALITY (ARTIFICIAL LIFE "IN SILICO")

Some silicon visionaries believe that natural evolution of the human species (or at least their branch of it) is near completion. They're interested in designing their successors.

Carnegie-Mellon robotics scientist Hans Moravec writes: "We owe our existence to organic evolution. But we owe it little loyalty. We are on the threshold of a change in the universe comparable to the transition from nonlife to life."

As flesh-and-blood species we are moribund, stuck at "a local optimum," to borrow a term from mathematical optimization theory. Human society is now reaching a turning point in the operation of the process of evolution, a point at which the next evolutionary step of the species will be under our control. Or more correctly, the next steps, which will occur in parallel, will result in an explosion of diversity of the human species. We shall no longer be dependent on fitness in any physical sense for survival. In the near future, computer and biological technologies will make the human form a matter totally determined by individual choice.

Beyond this horizon lies the unknown, the as yet scarcely imagined. We will design our children and coevolve intentionally with the cultural artifacts that are our progeny.

Humans already come in some variety of races and sizes. In comparison to what "human" will mean within the next century, we humans are at present as indistinguishable from one another as are hydrogen molecules. As we become conscious of this, our anthropocentrism will decrease.

I see two principal forms of the near-future human: the "cyborg," a bio/machine hybrid in any desired form, and the "postbiological," an electronic life-form on the computer networks. Human-as-machine and human-in-machine.

Of these, human-as-machine is perhaps more easily conceived. Today, we already have crude prosthetic implants, artificial limbs, valves, and entire organs. The continuing improvements in the old-style mechanical technology slowly increase the thoroughness of human-machine integration.

The electronic life-form of human-in-machine is even more alien to our current conceptions of humanity. Through storage of one's belief systems as online data structures, driven by selected control structures (the electronic analog to will?), one's neuronal apparatus will operate in silicon as it did on the wetware of the brain, although faster, more accurately, more self-mutably, and—if desired—forever.

ARCHIVAL, INFORMATIONAL IMMORTALITY

A digital age extension of a well-established way of becoming "immortal" is by leaving a trail of archives, biographies, tapes, films, computer files, and publicized noble deeds.

The increasing presence of reliable information media with high-storage capacity in our cybernetic society makes this a more rigorous platform for persistent existence. The knowledge possessed by an individual is captured in expert systems, and global-scale hypertext systems like the World Wide Web give the digital persona a connectedness and holism previously unimaginable.

Rudy Rucker is a great enthusiast for this form of personal immortality. In *MONDO 2000: A User's Guide to the New Edge,* he says, "I'm trying to merge my life with my fiction and essentially create a word model of my consciousness. If your brain software, your collected work, is on the disc, the computer can simulate you and you will be, in some sense, alive inside the computer." In an interview published in *21•C* magazine, he further conjectures about robots that could receive a person's personality. "You would first need a database. You would need to be interrogated over a long period of time. I think that some product might be available in about ten years that would follow you around, and it would ask you questions. It would generate this hypertext file. It might be called a lifebox. You'd give it to your grandchildren and they can say 'Did you ever play baseball, Grandpa?' and it would tell them. It will be a hypertext memoir. If it's done well enough you can actually talk to the person. . . . If a robot is complicated enough, it might be in some sense conscious."

Viewed from outside the self, death is not a binary phenomenon, but a continuously varying function. How alive is Shakespeare or Freud right now, as compared to the average citizen of each of their worlds?

NANOTECH INFORMATION STORAGE: DIRECT BRAIN-COMPUTER TRANSFER

When a computer becomes obsolete, one does not discard the data it contains. The hardware is merely a temporary vehicle of implementation for structures of information. The data gets transferred to new systems for continued use. Decreasing costs of computer storage and memory systems ensure that no information generated today need ever be lost.

One near-future projection involves our building an artificial computation substrate both functionally and structurally identical to the brain (and perhaps the body) of a person. How? Via the predicted future capabilities of nanotechnology. Networked nanomachines that pervade the organism may analyze the neural and cellular structure and transfer their findings to machines capable of growing, atom by atom, an identical copy.

But what of the soul? According to the *American Heritage Dictionary,* the soul is "the animating and vital principle in human beings credited with the faculties of thought, action, and emotion and often conceived as forming an immaterial entity."

At first, this definition seems like classic theological nonsense. But seen in the context of information theory, we may be able to wrestle this religiobabble into scientific operations. Let's change the bizarre word "immaterial" to "invisible to the naked eye," i.e., atomic-molecular-electronic. Now the "soul" refers to information processed and stored in microscopic cellular, molecular, atomic packages. Soul becomes any information that "lives," that is capable of being retrieved and communicated. From this viewpoint, our technological preservations are understood as cybernetic methods of preserving one's unique signal capacity. There are as many souls as there are ways of storing and communicating data. Tribal lore defines the racial soul. The DNA is a molecular soul. The brain is a neurological soul. Electron storage creates the silicon soul. Nanotechnology will make possible the atomic soul.

COMPUTER VIRAL EXISTENCE: GIBSON'S CYBERSPACE MATRIX

The nanotech option would permit personal survival through isomorphic mapping of neural structures to silicon or some other medium. It also suggests the possibility of survival as an entity in what amounts to a reflection of Jung's collective unconscious: the global information network.

In the twenty-first century imagined by William Gibson, wily cybernauts will not only store themselves electronically, but do so in the form of "computer viruses" capable of traversing computer networks and capable of self-replicating as a guard against accidental or malicious erasure by other persons or programs. (Imagine the somewhat droll scenario: "What's on the DUD-Ram?" "Ah, that's just old Leary. Let's go ahead and reformat it.")

Given the ease of copying computer-stored information, one could exist simultaneously in many forms. Where the "I" is in this situation is a matter for philosophy. I conjecture that consciousness would persist in each form, running independently, cloned at each branch point.

This list of options for voluntary, reversible metabolic coma and autometamorphosis is not mutually exclusive. The intelligent person needs little encouragement to explore all of these possibilities and to design many other new alternatives to going belly-up.

The viewpoint that now takes for granted the perishable, disposable human body-soul will soon be seen as historical barbarism. Individuals and groups will be free to reassume body-brain form, reconstructed by the appropriate sciences.

CHAPTER 12

The Cryonics Option

PASCAL IS FAMOUS FOR HIS STREET-SMART, RACE-track advice: "Bet that God exists. You can't lose." Today's hot tip: "Bet that future genetic technology will produce options for rebirth. You can't lose." In other words, you may want to take advantage of the nascent opportunity to have yourself preserved for possible future action.

Although I have chosen to move on, I encourage others to consider cryonics as the only current reanimation technique wherein the continuous "I" returns with (possibly) memories intact.

I've been saying that cryonics is the second dumbest thing I've ever heard of, next to dying. Indeed, it's possible to consider the individual hibernating in cryonic suspension not dead on a theoretical level. This is, at the very least, a conceptual breakthrough of enormous proportions.

A Glorious Experiment

The medical and scientific communities would label de- and reanimation an "experimental procedure." It may not work. If you sign up with a cryonics group, you will be part of the experiment to see if it actually does.

There are reasons for hope regarding the efficacy of low-temperature preservation. In the 1980s, a two-and-a-half-year-old girl who had been suspended in freezing cold water for over an hour was successfully resuscitated by a heart-lung machine with no ill effects. Human embryos have been frozen, revived, reimplanted, and birthed. (Lawsuits proliferate on the issue of who gets custody of the child.) Several dogs have been brought to a near-frozen state, with the loss of heartbeat, and revived. Recently a successful brain aneurysm operation was performed on a human who was cooled to 15 degrees centigrade.

Mainline cryobiologists are skeptical about the likelihood of human revival, since they focus on the noticeable damage done by cryonic freezing. This cynicism, though, has to be seen as reflecting the blindness of specialists. They have not considered the possibility of subsequent damage repair. This hope is currently offered by the science of nanotechnology. There is every reason to assume that other theoretical and practical scientific procedures for undoing damage will follow. There's ample reason to believe that low-temperature hibernation (what some wags have called "corpsicles") is the best avenue for eventual reanimation.

YOUR CRYONICS TEAM

The payoff for the cryonics organization occurs at the moment you pass over and they get to do their emergency response thing. Your cryonics team will jump into action, appearing at your bedside as swiftly as possible. Your body is put into an ice bath, where medications and a heart-lung resuscitator are used to restore breathing and blood circulation. This is done to prevent brain damage, which would otherwise occur due to lack of oxygen. (This may have the happy side effect of prolonging your after-death trip, as discussed in

Chapter 8). Then your blood temperature will be reduced to slightly above the freezing point of water. Finally, all your blood will be drained and replaced with an organ preservation fluid similar to that used for preserving donor organs during transportation. Your body is packed in ice, and off you go to the lab.

At the cryonics lab, the organ preservation fluids are replaced with an antifreeze agent. This will reduce negative effects of the freezing process on your cells. After a few days, your body temperature will be reduced to −196 centigrade, the temperature of liquid nitrogen. Finally, it's moved to a flask filled with liquid nitrogen. You will be stored head down (in case of accidental thawing you will lose your feet first). That's where you'll stay, doing a headstand and awaiting resurrection.

Or Just Take Along Your Brain

The option exists to freeze only your brain. The presumption here is that the technology will eventually exist to clone you a new body, or that your brain would be installed into the fully functioning body of a young person who has suffered brain death.

Brain preservation is cheaper than whole-body suspension. Focusing on the brain also allows for the optimal use of protectants during suspension. Cryonicists can concentrate all their efforts on just one organ rather than several. The brain is also a small mobile unit, easy to store. Just keep it on the mantle, or put it on top of the TV . . . but don't knock it over!

The idea of keeping someone's head in suspension pushes people's taboo buttons even more than whole-body suspension, which is one fun reason to *do* it. Saul Kent, one of the earliest supporters of cryonics and life extension, was arrested in a colorful case in which the head of his mother, Dora Kent, was taken off for cryonic suspension. The Los Angeles coroner's office decided that his mother had not been legally dead when her head was severed from her body and iced. The coroner wanted the cryonics company involved, ALCOR, to hand over the head, which would have effectively killed off Ms. Kent for all eternity. ALCOR evaded this. So the coroner's deputies, L.A. police, and a SWAT team invaded ALCOR's headquarters, removing all computing equipment, magnetic media, and prescription medications used for suspensions.

Eventually, after years of legal entanglements, the Dora Kent case slipped into oblivion. Dora's head still remains frozen, ready to tell us how it all looked from her perspective when she's reanimated.

WHY NOT BRAIN BANKS?

We now have heart banks. These are places where healthy hearts of people who've undergone brain death are stored before being given to people with healthy brains who need hearts. We have kidney banks, liver banks, lung banks, pancreas banks, eye banks, skin banks, tissue banks, bone banks, and DNA banks. I suggest that there will soon be brain banks. In fact, the brain is much easier to store than the heart. The heart has all those muscles. And think of the kidneys with all that plumbing to maintain. The brain, on the other hand, has no mechanical parts. It has almost no hardware to worry about. The brain should be easy to store.

Now, if I donated my brain to a bank, I could suggest the parameters for the person I want to give my brain to. I want my brain to be put into a beautiful, young, black woman. Imagine a young healthy black woman running around with Timothy Leary's brain and memories. (I could finally get through immigration and into the United Kingdom!)

MEMORIES CAN WAIT

Memories are most likely stored in molecular combinations in the brain. The question is how they can be recovered.

Neurologists claim that brain tissue that's suspended in liquid nitrogen can survive centuries without any signs of deterioration. The big hurdle in terms of bringing back brain function is freezer damage. While there's no reason to believe that a cure for freezer damage would violate any laws of physics, it seems that this repair is beyond the recovery capacities of the brain tissue itself. Therefore the possibility of full or partial restoration of brain function containing personality and memories rests on a technical intervention that can repair the damaged brain cells. Freezing yourself is basically a bet that a technology will evolve that can deal with this problem. Since it's reasonable to presume that there will be at least one or two generations of caretakers nurturing your frozen old head, the issue becomes whether it's reasonable to expect such a technology to be in place within the next fifty to one hundred years. The answer is a resounding YES! The reason for this hope is nanotechnology, which we will discuss in the next chapter.

What Price Immortality?

Immortality's cheaper than buying a house, even in the sticks! Whole-body preservation costs anywhere from $75,000 to $150,000. That covers preservation and maintenance. Brain preservation costs between $30,000 and $50,000. As you can see, consumer immortality is now an option for the middle class.

CRYONICS RESOURCES

Below are some cryonics foundations that you can contact, if you wish to investigate this option. CryoCare is the organization that Timothy Leary was signed with.

CryoCare Foundation
10627 Youngworth Road
Culver City, CA 90230
(800) 867–2273 (800–TOP–CARE)

Email: *cryonews@phantom.com* for both general information about CryoCare and also back issues of *CryoCare Report.*

ALCOR Life Extension Foundation
7895 East Acoma Dr., Suite 110
Scottsdale, AZ 85260
(602) 922–9013, (800) 367–2228
FAX (602) 922–9027
www: http://www.alcor.org
Email: *info@alcor.org*

Cryonics magazine, monthly, $25/yr. USA, $35/yr. Canada & Mexico, $40/yr. overseas ($10/yr. USA gift subscription for new subscriber)

(The American Cryonics Society is the membership organization and the suspensions and caretaking are done by Trans Time.)

American Cryonics Society (ACS)
P.O. Box 1509
Cupertino, CA 95015
(408) 734–4111
FAX (408) 973–1046, 24-hr. FAX (408) 255–5433
Email: *cryonics@netcom.com*

Supporting membership, including *American Cryonics* and *American Cryonics News,* $35/yr. USA, $40/yr. Canada & Mexico, $71/yr. overseas

Trans Time, Inc.
10208 Pearmain St.
Oakland, CA 94603
510–639–1955
Email: *quaife@math.berkeley.edu*

International Cryonics Foundation
1430 N. El Dorado
Stockton, CA 95202
(209) 463–0429
(800) 524–4456

Cryonics Institute (CI)
24355 Sorrentino Court
Clinton Township, MI 48035
Phone/FAX (810) 791–5961
Email: *cryonics@msn.com* or *ettinger@aol.com*

COMING BACK FROM LONG, LONG AGO

Consider the Egyptian pharaohs and their extraordinary preservation practice—mummification. This was the cryonics of their time. And they did such an extraordinary job that we find them, to this day, well preserved. Someday soon—and this is really quite likely—we may be able to clone the pharaohs because they've preserved their DNA. The pharaohs *made it!*

CHAPTER 13

Nanotechnology

FOR THOSE OF YOU WHO'VE BEEN LIVING IN A CAVE or are understandably overwhelmed by info overload, nanotechnology is the inexpensive and complete control over the structure of matter. It's the manipulation of matter, molecule by molecule. The advent of nanotechnology will result in the human ability to create limitless amounts of any substance consistent with the laws of the universe.

A nanometer is a millionth of a millimeter. This is hundreds of times smaller than a wavelength of light. With nanotechnology, we're talking about the construction of mechanical devices of this scale. As we will see later in this chapter, we're quickly working our way down toward having the ability to manipulate on that scale.

The potential of nanotechnology is awesome. With its success, the world could be a place of unimaginable economic bounty. It would, for instance, be possible to nearly automatically create any desired manufactured article from dirt and sunlight. Cellular repair machines embedded in every cell in the human body could retard or reverse the effects of aging and disease. Jet engines could be built in moments, grown as seamlessly and perfectly as crystals, from liquid solutions containing nanomachines, ad infinitum.

Nanotechnology would decentralize economics or, some would say, eliminate it as a factor in the human experience. On-site personal manufacturing stations would virtually eliminate mass production. Only slightly more subtle is the likelihood of extreme societal fragmentation due to the diversity of human form nanotechnology permits.

Nanomachines could effect transformation of human DNA, enabling eugenic customization. Radical human/machine hybrids could be developed through incorporation of nano-engineered mechanical componentry into the body, enabling total cosmetic reengineering of the human form to suit whim.

A Brief History of Nanotechnology

Ed Regis has written a wonderful book, *Nano,* that tracks the process by which scientists and engineers are gaining ever greater knowledge and control over ever smaller particles of matter. The book also follows the life-in-advocacy of K. Eric Drexler, the somewhat self-educated generalist-engineer who conceived the likely end result of this technical process in the late 1970s, naming it "nanotechnology." *Nano* is not the usual visionary science story about overoptimistic projections and crash landings. In fact, this is a story about discoveries and engineering feats that happen far more quickly than expected and that exceed all expectations. It's a story riddled with the red-faced conversions of nearly all the conservative, well-respected, skeptical scientists who take a closer look.

Journeying with Ed Regis through *Nano,* all but the most committed cynic will come to the same conclusion he does. Nanotechnology isn't just likely—it's more or less here now. But the road to nanotech has been littered with doubts and doubters. It all started with a talk by physics superstar Richard Feynman at the American Physical Society back in

1959 entitled "There's Always Room at the Bottom." Feynman asked, "Why cannot we write the entire twenty-four volumes of the *Encyclopaedia Britannica* on the head of a pin?" His argument revolved around the manipulation of atoms. It also presaged the basic argument raised by Drexler in favor of molecular technology. That argument, in simple terms, is "If nature can do it, why can't we?" At the end of his talk, Feynman offered a reward to "the first guy who can take the information on the page of a book and put it on an area 1/25,000 smaller in linear scale in such a manner that it can be read by an electron microscope." A substantial portion of Feynman's audience of educated scientists thought that either Mr. Feynman had gone completely daft or that the talk was a put-on. Feynman would live long enough to pay the $1,000 reward and, in fact, to see IBM scientists spell out "IBM" with thirty-five individual atoms of xenon.

The race to "the bottom," the search for knowledge of—and control over—ever smaller particles of matter, continued across the subsequent decades. This rapid trajectory toward nanotech has been propelled by a series of unexpectedly quick successes.

In 1980, Hans Dehmelt, a physics professor at the University of Washington, stunned the scientific world when he trapped a single atom inside a complex system of lasers. In 1984, he trapped a positron.

In 1981, Drexler talked about designing proteins and building them to order as one of the most important steps toward nanotechnology. He admitted that this difficult problem could be decades away from resolution. In 1987, Du Pont scientist William DeGrado, explicitly influenced by Drexler's book *The Engines of Creation,* actually did the deed. He declared that protein engineering "will allow us to think about designing molecular devices in the next five to ten years."

The invention of the Scanning Tunnel Microscope in

the early 1980s provided the tool needed for the manipulation of atoms. In 1987, Todd Gustavson, an eighteen-year-old Californian built his own in his father's workshop. It cost him $200. The specter of garage nanotechnology—nanopunk—is already an issue among the nano conscious. And if you think that computer viruses are troublesome, imagine a self-replicating material-object generator that can't be turned off. This is what's known as the "grey goo" problem among nanoheads, the charming idea being that the entire world would quickly be buried underneath, say . . . self-replicating pie filling.

By 1994, in Regis's words, "the atomic realm had been colonized by a weird assortment of manmade shapes, structures, materials, and devices. There were atomic switches, self-replicating molecules, and molecular shuttles and trains . . . buckyballs, nanotubes, atomic corrals, nanowires, and molecular propellers and gears. There were deliberately engineered artificial proteins, faux-proteins, and even artificial atoms." Nanotechnology is more or less a fact of life. Although Drexler's cornucopian molecular machines still await construction, even his harshest critic in the field, the ever courageous "anonymous," who had earlier called Drexler a flake and his notions "science fiction" and "pure hype," had to admit recently, "There's more to this than I thought."

Bringing Back the Dead: Cryonics and Nanotechnology

Understand that nanotechnology, programming and building stuff molecule by molecule, is what nature does. So it makes sense that molecular machines can build cells (including brain cells) from scratch. Cell division demonstrates this. The development of embryos shows us that nanotech can build us organs. In the future, we'll have replaceable parts. Who wouldn't want to have a fresh young heart or a brand-new liver? Or who wouldn't like to repair a few brain cells? Especially us!!!

Neurobiology has given us the good news. Memory and personality are set in preservable brain structures. The marvelous two-hundred-billion-neuron network in our heads functions by molecular machinery. As Eric Drexler has put it, "Lasting changes in brain function involve lasting changes in this molecular machinery—unlike a computer's memory, the brain is not designed to be wiped clean and refilled at a moment's notice. Personality and long-term memory are durable."

In other words, our future claims to individuality don't have to rely completely on our pretty faces. Memory and personality are contained in the way that brain cells have evolved patterns based on each of our experiences. Memory and personality don't expire the very second that you do. Biochemists and other scientists tell us that we'll be able to intervene in cross-linked structures and repair damaged cells. In all likelihood, presuming nanotechnology, we can come back at 100 percent, just like Woody Allen in *Sleeper.* All the recent explorations into neurology support the notion that memories, in fact, *can* wait.

CHAPTER 14

The Twenty-first Century: Cyborgization and Postbiological Immortality Options

Through science and technology we will meet the aliens, and they will be us.

NORMAN SPINRAD, *THE NEUROMANTICS*

I'd like to be a machine.

ANDY WARHOL

FINALLY, WE LOOK TOWARD THE TWENTY-FIRST century at options that many of you reading this may face within your life spans. In Chapter 11, we touched on the two possible types of future humans, cyborgs and postbiologicals. The possibilities not only for infinite immortality but for reconfiguration of one's organism make *Hitchhiker's Guide to the Galaxy*'s twin-headed Zaphod BeebleBrox seem tame. Desire another eye? No problem. Simply swallow the capsule containing the self-replicating nanocomputers that tamper with the metabolism of cells throughout your organism to affect the desired embellishment.

Future Life-forms in Sterling's *Schismatrix*

The most thoughtful and concise envisioning of where future cyborgian and postbiological experimentation will likely take us was offered by Bruce Sterling's seminal early cyberpunk novel *Schismatrix*. In this book, Sterling recognizes the fact that human evolution moves in many directions, not along a single path. His "Mechs" and "Shapers" correspond closely with our notions of electronic and biogenetic paths to evolutionary diversity.

In *Schismatrix,* Sterling refers to humanity's successors as "clades," a biological term meaning "daughter species." The posthuman clades differ in their cultural and social organization, but especially in their preferred technologies. The initial division is between Mechanists (who use robotics and AI) and Shapers (who use bio- and psychotechnology). Eventually there are additional posthuman beings representing new modes of existence ("star-peering wireheads").

A clade would not be an eternally separate entity, however. Just as humans will become transhumans and posthumans, so one might transform oneself and pass from Mechanist to Shaper. In Sterling's future, clades form distinct societies, but in a "trans-cladistic" future such differences of form might represent nothing more than an accommodation made to a local culture (when on Jupiter, live as the Jovians do).

From Cyborg to Postbiot

Consider the following thought experiment:

The time is today. Our hero, undeniably human, conscious, and alive, goes to his physician suffering from a mild but persistent hearing impairment. The physician, up-to-date in the latest methods of neuroscience, suggests that the offending nerve be replaced by a small and unobtrusive piece of microelectronic equipment, a nerve-splicer. The tiny device can be implanted in the patient's ear to bypass the faulty nerve and will restore his hearing to normal.

The operation is completed, and the implanted device functions as intended: effectively and unobtrusively. Unarguably, our soon-to-be-bionic hero is every bit as human as before the operation. A few years later, in an automobile accident, he suffers a head injury. Fortunately for him, medical science has advanced still further, to the point where the damaged nervous tissue can be functionally augmented by another similarly small and unobtrusive implanted device. The happy fellow returns to his normal life, for all purposes unchanged by the natural and unnatural circumstances that have befallen him.

Over the years, more and more pieces of our protagonist are replaced by artificial components that mimic perfectly the function of the tissues they replace. He wakes up one morning to the startling revelation that he's entirely artificial. Gradually, all of the protein-based tissue that he was born with has been replaced by functionally identical artificial parts. He is what could only be called a machine, a robot.

Yet, examining his situation, he realizes he's every bit as consciously alive and human as he ever was. Was there some point where the spark of his humanity dimmed, denying him human status? Reflect on his situation as he does. With his essentially *Homo sapien* brain, he can remember no critical small part whose replacement caused the flame of his consciousness to be snuffed out.

Imagine the following even weirder scenario. As the techniques of biological engineering continue to advance, it's not implausible that RNA-based biomachines will be designed to act as computer subsystems to perform specific tasks.

The current popularity of the neural net approach to computation, coupled with molecular engineering, suggests that artificial biological nets may soon be grown for use within conventional computers.

The silicon-based architecture of our present-day computers may be transmuted over time to result in completely biological robots. Should these creatures be accorded animal rights? If they show sentience, should they be accepted as human? (Programming "emotional responses"—likes and dislikes—is already central to the success of companies like Wildfire who provide personal-assistant software/serviceware to the corporate elite.)

Uploading: Mind if I Slip into Something More Incorruptible?

The most commonly discussed mode for postbiological living is the idea of uploading, copying or otherwise somehow transferring, your brain patterns and structures onto a new format, probably a highly advanced computer hybrid.

Hans Moravec is the most well known proponent of this future technology. In his book *Mind Children,* Moravec suggests a gradual transference of consciousness into steady state, neuron by neuron. According to Extropian Eliezer Yudkowsky, this might be accomplished by a process in which nanotechnological robots scan each of the brain's neurons, placing a copy on the hard drive of the computer.

THE SMALLER YOU BRAIN, THE FASTER YOU THINK

If making backup copies of your consciousness isn't a big enough kick to get you fired up for the future, consider the possibility that you might also get a supersonic brain! According to Drexler, the structure of the brain will be miniaturized to less than a cubic centimeter. Shorter signal paths combined with speedier transmission will yield a posthuman postbrain that operates millions of times faster than the current model.

HOW DO WE GET BRAINS ON A CHIP?

As I've already indicated, current postbiological theorists believe we'll scan our neurological patterns in. Uploading will involve making a detailed copy of the morphology of the neural tissue. Scientists are currently looking toward electron microscopy (EM), X-ray holography, and optical interferometry as concrete methods to achieve this aim.

Alternatively, scientists are looking at neural networks—artificial systems that function similarly to neurons. Reports from the neurosciences give hope that here is yet another area where we will likely see the functional duplication of brain circuitry.

THE BRAIN CHIPS AREN'T DOWN AND OTHER EVOLUTIONARY TRENDS

Currently, research is moving ahead on computer-brain interfaces. A number of scientists are attempting to create computer-chip matrices into which nerves can grow. This would allow communication between neurons and computers. These technologies are already being applied to peripheral nerves and the control of prosthetic instruments.

Still further progress is occurring in electronic prosthetics for sight and hearing—optic nerve interfaces and cochlear implants. With the progress in biological computing and storage media, there appears to be an inevitable confluence between organic computing, neural network software, and neural-computer interfaces. The distinction between brain and computer is breaking down, with the boundaries between human and machine eroding to yield an eventual biological/hardware hybrid.

Also, a recent article in *Scientific American* predicts the advent of protein-based computers. Cubes of this material would be able to store nearly a hundred trillion bits per cubic centimeter (compared to about a hundred million bits per in two-dimensional media).

UPLOADING PROCEDURES

The most immediately thinkable procedure for uploading is called the microtome procedure. This generally involves a cryonically preserved brain. The brain is sliced thin. Each slice is scanned into a computer using an electron microscope. The computer reconstructs the brain's circuitry onto some form of hardware.

Like the microtome procedure, uploading techniques originally suggested by Hans Moravec and others involve the destruction of the actual physical brain as it was transferred into solid state. Naturally, other scientists and thinkers have suggested less drastic procedures involving copying the brain for uploading. Some suggested methods include:

- *Correlation mapping:* Here, nanoscale probes are injected into the cerebrospinal fluid to monitor random neurons. The probe is designed to secrete a chemical binary code regarding the current state of the host brain cell. Over time, enough information is gathered about relations between cell states to map the activity of a specific brain.
- *Gamma-ray holography:* A gamma-ray source makes a three-dimensional recording of the brain structure with near-atomic resolution.
- *MRI (magnetic resonance imaging):* This technique is used to cause the brain to emit radio waves. These are collected and analyzed to produce a three-dimensional atomic-scale map of the brain.

BRAIN ON CHIPS: IS THIS THE TASTIEST SOLUTION?

The question remains, if you could upload into solid state, would you want to? Is uploading a good alternative to shucking this earthly existence? And further, since many advanced neophiles are prepared to upload copies of themselves while still living, is it a good ride? We can only conjecture that consciousness free of its earthly bounds, involved in traversing virtual worlds in a computer matrix, or perhaps moved into other forms ranging from humanoid robot to currently unimaginable mechanical/biological hybrids, would experience a kind of bliss. Recall that we are discussing a solution that includes a speeding up of neural processes with nearly unlimited learning and intelligence. And as any veteran of consciousness drugs can tell you—my God, even methamphetamine or cocaine—a well lit up, fast-moving brain *feels good.*

CHAPTER 15

Timothy Leary's Final Escape

BY R. U. SIRIUS

I think Mister Newton has had enough.

THE MAN WHO FELL TO EARTH, FINAL LINE

IT CERTAINLY WOULD HAVE BEEN GRAND *GUIGNOL.* The media would have gone nuts, wouldn't they have? Not only was Timothy Leary going to choose the cryonics option, he let it drop that he might deanimate live on the Internet, before an audience of millions.

But in the end, Tim Leary made a choice to leave this mortal coil behind, quietly with family and friends, forever . . . no deposit, no return.

Stories abound about fighting between Leary and his inner circle and the folks from the cryonics group CryoCare, who would have been the ones to hold the famous soul on ice in anticipation of advanced scientific rejuvenation techniques. From one side we hear that Tim and his companions wouldn't abide by the basic rules of preparation necessary for the moment of suspension. On the other side, we hear that the cryonics enthusiasts were poised like vultures awaiting Leary's death, that they were uptight about the way Tim's young artist friends had turned the cryonics chamber into a pagan shrine, that they were preachy and disapproving. I've chosen not to investigate this soap opera, as I don't think it was the major factor in his decision.

Tim certainly *did* say that he didn't want to "wake up in fifty years surrounded by humorless men with clipboards." And it was obvious, in his last years, that he preferred the company of his young and old bohemian friends (holding frequent phone conversations with William S. Burroughs and Hunter Thompson) to the rather straight cryonics types. And I'm sure that influenced his decision. But finally, I think it can be stated simply—Timothy Leary had had enough. He told Ken Kesey, "I've exhausted this planet's particular pleasures."

Tim wouldn't want this put in a negative light. The man loved life, every last second of it. But he was also tired. After all, he had packed quite a few extra lifetimes into his seventy-six years. He'd reexperienced all of evolution from the Precambrian slime to the ultimate union with galactic central on what was—for the rest of us—many a normal afternoon. He'd spent some time in society's courtrooms playing the heretic, done some four years in prison, been controversial and in trouble for several decades. He'd experienced the grief of a wife's and a daughter's suicide and left behind an angry son with whom there would be no reconciliation. He'd been hounded by the CIA, the DEA, and the Nixon White House. His countercultural reputation had been badly damaged by the California judicial system and the FBI. His last wife, of fourteen years, Barbara, had left him. He'd written entire eschatologies, psychological systems, and evolutionary road maps—none of which got as much attention as they deserved. All the while, he maintained a successful career as a public speaker, became one of L.A.'s most fabled "A list" party animals, and stayed on top of all the latest developments in science, technology, and culture. He'd remained upbeat, encouraging, and anti-authoritarian. He continued to cheer on those around him, always embracing novelty, giving his thumbs-up to the latest technological hacks and youth culture trends. He was probably the most active and subversive seventy-six-year-old presence on the World Wide Web.

Leary said several times that he wasn't really all that anxious to return. His plans for cryonic preservation were intended as a symbolic gesture, encouraging people to investigate alternatives to "involuntary dying." But whether it was Harvard, the peace movement, Eldridge Cleaver, the California penal system, or the Extropian movement (advocates of cryonics and nanotechnology), Tim Leary didn't like to be a captive pawn in anybody else's game. And so he escaped. Once again.

> What is the way of the Tao? Move on!
>
> LAO-TZU

ADDENDUM

Timothy Leary's Dying Performance as Remembered by His Friends

Introduction by R. U. Sirius

TIMOTHY LEARY WAS AN ENIGMATIC MAN. BLINDINGLY charismatic, he radiated like a glowing sun . . . *most of the time.* The first time I met him, in Rochester, New York, in 1980, I was high for several weeks. He could make you feel life was a great party that was only going to get better. As I got to know him better, that impression remained. Here was a person of extraordinary generosity, a true "people person" who went out of his way to make people feel happy, alive, and interested *most of the time.*

But there was another Timothy Leary, one who would come out some of the time, frequently during the question-and-answer part of public appearances. This Timothy Leary was impatient and snippy. He'd force a smile, but he really wanted to end the public discourse and head for the bar with the prettiest girl in the audience. I was one of the lucky few (thousand) who got to hang with that Leary and learned to love this aspect of his humanness. I suppose that I came to California half expecting to get to know this eight-circuits-high psychedelic superman, someone *totally* together, making the future while in a state of perpetual, functional bliss. But I was actually relieved to discover a fellow flawed human being. And Tim made damn sure that you *had* to accept him flawed, or not at all.

Then there was the angry Timothy Leary. Being an old Yippie! anti-authoritarian conceptual-bomb thrower myself, I always loved that one. You couldn't miss the fiery Irish revolutionary temper lurking right behind the broad smile and the gentle reassurances that we humans were on the verge of getting it just right. I was delighted that during the 1980s and 1990s anti-authoritarianism became his number-one message. And I felt a tremendous loss in the early 1990s as his incredible intellectual sharpness began to wane. Who would we send up against the William Bennetts and the Rush Limbaughs now that we didn't have Leary at his peak? He felt the loss too. He once phoned me in 1991 to say that he was going to "deamimate" soon, because his brain wasn't functioning at 100 percent. That's how deeply he felt his responsibility to be an effective communicator.

Finally, there was the Tim Leary that was most hidden from the public eye—a sad old guy, a blues person. Meeting *that* Timothy Leary remains my fondest memory. We had gone to a party at the house where Sharon Tate had been murdered by the Anti-Tim of the LSD culture, Charles Manson, and his followers. Trent Reznor was now occupying the place. Talk about your strange resonances—tripping with Tim (and Simone Third Arm) on Ecstasy in this haunted house would seemingly qualify as an episode in the World Series of psychedelic weirdness. But when we entered the party to find Reznor and other partyers (I'll spare you an orgy of name dropping) munching on magic mushrooms, the weirdest thing imaginable occurred. *Nothing!* That is . . . no spooky vibes. The sad terror of Sharon Tate didn't visit us. The dark cosmic ego of Charles Manson didn't visit us. We were, in fact, in the middle of an extraordinarily sweet party filled with high, sophisticated conversation that drifted from the nature of the universe to the ups and downs of the interaction between creative people and the entertainment industry. As we left the party in high spirits, I became dimly aware that Tim Leary's presence had been keeping the spirit aloft.

We returned to Tim's house. He poured wine for everybody. He put on a Billie Holiday CD, lit a fire, and sat down next to it. Simone draped her arm around him lovingly. He said in a quiet voice, "I'm going to take a Valium. Does anybody else want one?" I looked at him and, suddenly, there was all the weariness and sadness from all the decades that this one small, embodied individual had carried the weight of attempting to transmute our sad old world into a place worthy of the highest psychedelic visions. I flashed on his daughter's recent suicide. And my thoughts lingered over the reality that it was *no joke* that here before me was Tim Leary, a man who had to—in some sense—carry the weight of the Charlie Manson bummer, a man who had been in a karma dance that involved Richard Nixon, the Vietnam war, the (in my opinion) even more devastating War on Drugs, and the tragedies that went along with the millions of illuminations that psychedelica had provided.

Tim Leary *had* been holding that night's party up on a positive high by the will of his own loving spirit and genial wit. He'd been holding the entire late-twentieth-century popular psychedelic culture party to essentially good-natured standards throughout increasingly mean-spirited times, without ever becoming pious or self-righteous. And here he was: human, tired, and singing a melancholy song about heartache along with Billie Holiday. In that moment, I really fell in love with Timothy Leary.

About the Addendum

While Leary was always a wonderful, witty writer, the warmth and generosity of his presence was not always available in his writing. The tech stuff could be a bit chilly. The anti-authority stuff could be pretty angry. When he spoke of Prison Earth or ridiculed the "lower-circuit" activities of our species, it could sometimes obscure the basic life-affirming, people-loving, fun-loving, impish spirit that was the absolute essence of Tim to those who knew him well. Especially in his last year-and-a-half display of amazing courage in the face of pain and death, his greatest teaching couldn't be found in a book or a lecture. It had to be experienced in person.

I wish I could take readers of this book back and let them spend time in the presence of Leary so they could absorb the full effect of his final act. Since that's not possible, I've done the next best thing. I've asked his closest friends from that period to describe their experience of him from that time. I asked them two questions: *"What was the lesson for you of Tim's performance of the dying process?"* and *"What's your favorite memory of Tim from that time?"* Some answered the questions straightforwardly, some threw the questions out the window and gave me something else, and others did a little of each. In any case, I consider this segment the most important part of the book. Somewhere within the multiperspective *Roshomon* chaos of these responses is Timothy Leary's true Design for Dying. In deference to the comments of Robert Anton Wilson (now the smartest man alive!) herein, I leave it to you to assign the meaning for yourselves.

JOHN PERRY BARLOW

Grateful Dead lyricist, writer, cyberculture spokesperson

Lesson: Of course, the manner of Tim's departure was his last and probably peskiest revolutionary act, a jubilantly rotten egg to splat on the smooth, humorless face of this culture's denial of death. But, aside from admiring it, I personally learned little from that. I'd already been taught my own related lessons.

I suppose the lesson he left with me was that it's never too late to come into a sense of the spirit, a perception he fiercely resisted all the years I knew him. As he drew near the membrane between this reality and the next, it seemed he could begin to peer through to the other side. He seemed comforted by what he saw, comforted enough to bet his immortality on that spiritual vision rather than the cryogeek's cold reason.

Favorite Memory: A few days before he died, we were driving around L.A. in a rented convertible. I was running errands and he came along for the ride. At one point, I ran into a store and left Tim in the car. When I returned, he was craned forward in his seat, closely examining his ravaged face in the side mirror.

But there was something about his expression—a kind of metaphysical humor that struck me. I watched him for a moment and suddenly realized that the joke arose from combining the immediate image of himself with the words printed on the base of the mirror: "Objects in mirror are closer than they appear." We both started to laugh and neither of us had to check with the other to know we were riding the same goof.

Please feel free to use the piece that I sent out over the Net when Tim died . . .

TIMOTHY LEARY'S DEAD

A couple of hours ago, at 12:45 A.M. Beverly Hills time, old friend and corrupter of my youth Timothy Leary made good on his promise to "give death a better name or die trying." Willingly, peacefully, and unafraid, he headed off on his last trip.

He spoke his last words a few hours before. On the phone to the mordant William S. Burroughs he said, "I hope that someday I'm as funny as you are."

He didn't, as threatened, commit suicide on the Net. Or have his head cut off and frozen. Or engage in any of the other spectacles of departure I had dreaded. In the end, he surrounded himself with the angelic band of twenty-somethings who have been uploading him into the Web these last few months and drifted peacefully out of here.

I was headed his way when he died. When I was with him earlier this month he said, "When I leave here, Barlow, I want your face to be one of the last things I see." I think that was one of the sweetest things anyone ever said to me, and I was trying to make it possible, but death proved itself once again to be bigger and faster than either of us. The phone just rang in the middle of this rainy Wyoming night, and now I'm here naked in the dark trying to think of something to follow him out with.

Two years ago, Cynthia [Barlow's "perfect love"] and I spent our last day together with Timmy. When she died the next day and it became so shockingly clear to both of us how strange this culture has become on the subject of the second commonest event in the world, how weirdly shameful is dying in America, we both thought it time to bring death out of the closet. I did so by grieving her, and continuing to grieve her, more publicly than is polite in a culture that claims for itself the ability to conquer and control everything.

But Timmy beat me to the barricades. He flat died. And he died without pretending that he was "really going to get well any day now," without permitting himself to become a ghoulish and futile medical experiment, without contributing to the stupefying mass denial that causes almost 80 percent of America's health-care dollars to be blown on the last six months of life.

He died unashamed and having, as usual, a great time.

A few weeks ago, the denizens of leary.com and I rented a phalanx of wheelchairs and rode them with him into the House of Blues on Sunset Strip, a place that likely had never seen fifteen people in wheelchairs before. After a truly merry time, we were headed back to his house and on the way came within a smile of Tim Leary's Last Bust.

We were cruising west on Sunset. And the sun was setting. The top was down on my metallic mauve rent-a-convertible. A couple of the Web girls, Trudy and Camilla, were sitting on the trunk like psychedelic prom queens, shoop-de-booping to the funk station on the radio, volume at eleven. Both of the girls were beautiful, Trudy like a character from *Neuromancer,* Camilla like a character from Botticelli. The air was sweet and soft as a negligee on our faces, and the light had that elegiac quality that makes people think L.A. might not be so bad after all.

Timmy gave me a high five and grinned. "Life is good!" he shouted over the music. As I looked up to meet his raised hand, I saw in my rearview mirror, past the swaying torsos of the girls, the rotating reds of a real Beverly Hills cop.

Of course we were in possession of several of those substances that we considered safe and effective but that this culture, in another of its dangerous madnesses, has declared lethal, probably to distract heat from its own deadly drugs of choice. Furthermore, I had only recently paid an astonishingly steep California fine for allowing a friend to stand up through the sunroof of a car I was driving.

He pulled us over in front of the Beverly Hills Hotel. He looked like an Eagle Scout.

"Officer," I said, nodding back at the still improperly seated girls, "I know what we were doing was wrong. But you see, my friend here is dying, and we're trying to show him a good time." Timmy, without saying anything, smiled sheepishly at the cop and nodded, caught in the act.

He looked like hell but he sure looked happy.

The officer gazed into Timmy's beatific

skull-face and lost his starch. "Well," he said to the girls, "I'd be lying if I didn't say that looks like fun, but just because he's dying doesn't mean you should. Now get down in the seat and buckle up and I'll let you go." I felt like honest death had just made one of its first converts.

In thirty years of following Tim Leary around, he's given me some wonderful and hair-raising moments. He has been father, anti-father, partner-in-crime, and devout fellow worshiper of all that is female in this world. We loved each other and shared more memories than I will ever relate. But I think the look he gave that cop is the memory I will cherish most.

As usual he was "cocking snooks at authority," as Aldous Huxley once accused him. But he was doing it, also as usual, with wit. And with love.

America managed to forgive Richard Nixon when he died. I hope they will extend the same amnesty to a real hero, Dr. Timothy Leary.

Pinedale, Wyoming
Friday, May 31, 1996

DENIS BERRY

Friend, former Dial-A-Wife

Lesson: We are not our bodies. During Tim's last days (weeks/months) I was amazed by the spirit of this man and tenacity of his frail little body. His body did gradually get weaker and weaker and, as he got less functional physically, his spirit and sheer will pushed a body that looked as if it should crumble at any moment. When he got too weak to walk, he'd drive his electric wheelchair as if he were Mario Andretti in a speed race. He would zoom down the hall, turn left through the living room, practically do a wheelie, and land in place at the table.

Particularly the last week of his life, he became so frail he was almost transparent. The day he died I held him in my arms and all that was left was skin and bones; but it was not until his spirit left that what had moments before been Timothy Leary laying on his bed was, indeed, now a *shell* . . . not the man I had known and loved.

Favorite Memory: My favorite times were the few times we got to be alone. One morning in particular, I was staying at the house overnight and we were out at the table on the patio, Tim with his newspaper and usual cup of coffee. We read the newspaper quietly for quite a while and then started reminiscing about the time we had spent together. We talked about the quiet evenings at home by ourselves, the openings we had attended and enjoyed, the evening at the House of Blues with Tom Davis. He told me how much he appreciated my friendship and I told him how much my life had been enriched by knowing him. I think it was one of the few heart-to-heart dialogues we ever had.

SARAH BROWN
Granddaughter

Lesson: The lesson for me was that everybody must and will die. To many, Timothy Leary was a god, but no man is immortal. So you must be careful in how you live, in what you do, and what you say, because you never know when your time is up.

Favorite Memory: It's hard to have a good memory of the death of someone you loved and looked up to. I'm just glad he died peacefully, around friends, and without any pain.

DAVID BYRNE

Musician, artist

Lesson: "Performance" might unintentionally be the right word here. Tim's whole adult life seemed to be a kind of performance, both in the Western theatrical sense and in the more Zen-type sense of seeing one's life as a kind of play . . . as if we are all acting out our roles in a purely subjective, artificial, and arbitrary reality.

In the former, Western, sense of performance, Tim, throughout his life, and even in the dying process, turned himself into a guinea pig on which he publicly exercised his own enthusiasms and interests . . . from drugs to software. His friends and the media were his audience. . . . He was always "on." And he seemed to thrive on it.

One could see both his life and his dying as a contemporary version of the medieval morality plays, popular entertainments that instructed and taught, although their lessons were very different from those of Dr. Tim. Even the endlessly long small-town productions of the *Ramayana* and the *Mahabharata* throughout Southeast Asia are a form of instruction and elucidation . . . clarifying one's place in the cosmos through hilarious and heroic examples. Tim's living and dying was like that to me . . . a sad but heroic performance that served as an example to contemplate and possibly emulate.

Favorite Memory: I wasn't in L.A. that much during Tim's last year. . . . We communicated by fax and phone during that period . . . but I remember one night when he was already ill joining him at a hip new restaurant/club of his choosing. . . . The other dinner guests were all fairly insane and fascinating from what I could gather over the pounding music. After a few hours I started to fade, but I looked over and Tim, already evidencing clear signs of illness, was going strong, making sure that everybody at the table knew what everybody's current projects were and what everyone else was up to. He was an endless promoter, not of himself (although that too), but of the work, enthusiasms, and creations of his friends. . . . He was a go-between who introduced people and characters who might not otherwise meet.

Seeing Tim there and remembering him like that, I didn't find it surprising that he would soon announce his dying performance, that he would revolutionize his and many others' approach to this ultimate trip. Odd coincidence too that Tim's old friend Ram Dass is currently very involved in counseling folks in the dying process.

DEAN CHAMBERLAIN
Photographer

How I Met Tim: I met Tim on February 18, 1996. It was the beginning of what I believe would have been a very long friendship. Our relationship was amplified by Tim's dying performance, and I immediately began collaborating with him on a photographic portrait of him in his home. We worked together selling editioned prints of this portrait as a way of raising money for his Web site project and personal needs.

Meanwhile, my wife, Stacy, and I took on a myriad of roles in Tim's life: nurse, aide, confidante. He even began to call me his "product guy," I suppose for my assuming the unlikely part of an impromptu business manager by way of the success in print sales.

As I became more aware of his ebbing cognitive skills, I introduced him to making "word drawings." I would stay up late in his bedroom, cheering him on and praying to myself that he would live long enough to see his works exhibited. These drawings are the creations of a dying genius wordsmith, whose mind was at one moment entirely lucid and at the next crumbling out from under him.

Lesson: My work has always been about light. Never did I expect to meet a human being who shone as brilliantly as he did for me. Tim's mind radiated through his words and eyes. Everyone's does, but with Tim it was like watching lightning. He electrified us until the moment he closed his eyes for the last time. It was a wordless yet divine communication, his mind spark-gapping into ours. A split-second glance transmitted a whole universe, a universe of light and intelligence.

The closer Tim got to death, the more I saw him take great pleasure in the wordlessness of illumination. It was as if he were sensing his own ascent into light and realized how the worded intellect may not be so valuable where he was going. Tim always understood how light is the life essence, and to that end he would let fly amazing wordplay to express his extensive understanding of LSD, computers, and dying. He even spoke about how word languages would someday give way to "species communication through specific and complex languages of light."

Tim's lucid mind delved deeply, instantaneously, and his brain would flash thoughts, ideas, jokes, and truths out at us without a moment's hesitation. His piercing mind was reflective of those around him. He communicated back to us our highest potential if we were open to it. With him we could see everything around us from a brilliant vantage point.

I once asked him how he regarded his ego. He said, "I don't have ego the way most people do." On the surface that might sound egotistical in itself, but I got the idea that Tim was born with two separate brains operating in tandem. One was his own, and the other was ours.

The final service he did us on his deathbed, just hours before his earthly end, made this dual brain and dual heart extraordinarily apparent. I lay sick with a blazing fever on the bed just outside his room, unable to even get up. There were close to twenty people sitting around Tim's bed in a loving and almost silent vigil. Everyone thought Tim had most likely said his last words and was moments from completely fading.

But to everyone's surprise, he opened his eyes and looked around the room at each and every person watching him. He managed to clap his hands very faintly as his eyes touched each person's. He was applauding US! No wallowing in self-pity for Tim, folks. Here, for me is the true mark of the man. He involved us in his earthly death. Even after that, he broadcast his five-minute mantralike repetition of "Why not?" sixty times. Where there was social taboo and fear, there was Tim cheering us on to break through. Then he went off to light and is still radiating inside me showing me my best moves. Tim is alive and well as light of the mind released from the dense realm. This light, purified of the fears and pains of death, has showed me where to aim. I imagine Tim dissolved into light, into the light that I will spend the rest of my life tuning into.

Favorite Memory: My most meaningful memory of Tim occurred two weeks before he died. It was in the wee hours, working on what turned out to be his last drawing.

He was using ketamine, enhanced by nitrous balloons from the tank by the bed. On the table before him was a sheet of multicolored and -faceted silver mylar. He struggled with the drawing for what seemed like an eternity. He was in some far-off land of his mind, hunched over, and nodding out intermittently. Then he'd suddenly "come back" and ask what we were doing.

"We're drawing, Tim," I'd tell him. Then he'd manage to put a few more meandering marks on the drawing surface before drifting off again. It was heart-wrenching to witness this. He wanted so desperately to be productive, yet had so little stamina or concentration left.

Then, suddenly, as if calling in from this far-off land,

he exclaimed, "My optic nerves are singing! I'm blinded by screaming tears! My God, the light coming off this drawing is blinding me! Its shimmering brilliance! It's almost too much for me!"

He looked up at me through his scratched and broken glasses. I saw tears welling in his eyes. I'll never forget that look. He was almost plaintive, as if I would be able to offer him guidance, but I was simply overwhelmed with my own helplessness. I had no guidance to offer. My heart broke. He was on a path alone and so was I. I sensed he had stared into the eyes of death. My empathy with his apparent need made me vulnerable to a fear I had never felt before. At this time I thought it was fear of death. Months later now, I realize Tim's silent plea for guidance was even more complex. It was Tim in his multifaceted self, reflected back to himself through that blindingly bright piece of mylar. Tim the child, the friend, the mentor, the philosopher, the psychologist, the lover, the one whose laugh and warmth lit up many people's hearts and minds—Tim in pain and ecstasy at the same moment. Perhaps he was hungry, or had to pee, or was tired, bored, or wanted to walk. All these Tims, and all these intentions, the infinite potential posed by an unflinchingly courageous being, were soon to cease. I must admit, I was not accepting this reality. I was having the time of my life playing the dying game with him.

ROBIN CHRISTIANSEN

Friend, massage therapist, artist

Lesson: I had the privilege of seeing the "real thing" close up for about five months before his death. I visited Tim once or twice a week to massage his weary bones—which the cancer had struck hard. He was in a lot of pain much of the time. He would only announce in plain sentences that he was in pain, matter-of-factly, and then not mention it at all for the remainder of the visit. This is one of the worst cancers you can get—when it begins to seep into the bones. Tim never really broke down. He always kept his head up. I learned the biggest lesson I could possibly learn, close up—to die with dignity. Tim was a true teacher/advocate/shaman to the very last day. He may have been afraid, but in all of the time I spent with him, he kept his pride, kept his charm, and kept everyone around him—sometimes to three in the morning, I heard—busy. He certainly showed me how to be brave and how to stay "really" alive even if death sometimes gets in the way. I feel very lucky to have known him for five years. He was a great star for us all!

Favorite Memory: I'm pretty lucky to have not only been able to massage Timothy—but to get my wish—to really get to know him on an intimate level—amidst the swirl of friends and associates permeating his life at all times! One favorite memory is an interview that friends of mine did—David J. Brown and Rebecca McClen, who coedited the book *Voices from the Edge,* among others. It was arranged during one of Tim's massage sessions. A few more of Tim's friends were visiting that night. They joined us and we all sat around Tim's bed while David and Rebecca interviewed away. We all sat around Tim like it was an impromptu gathering, and Tim got his feet massaged for a whole hour. Every so often he would squeal out in ecstasy from my treatment as he simultaneously entertained everybody with jokes and smiles and answered all of David's questions. Definitely a cherished evening for all of us.

The other great memento, for me, was the night Nina Graboi was visiting Tim for the weekend and brought with her some special brownies she baked for Tim. In the middle of his treatment Tim wanted another cookie—told me which drawer to look in—and to bring him one. So into his mouth it went, and as I leaned over to rub away, he, circa 1967, put a small piece in my mouth. My other wish: to share a Timothy Leary psychedelic moment! It wasn't too long before I was floating around the house hunting down Nina Graboi to thank her. I was suddenly mesmerized by her—helping make up her bed in Tim's office—and learning that Nina felt like she was the yin to Tim's yang. I like to think I never came down from that one. What a nice gift to get high with Tim and thank Nina—the 1960s queen of the flower children herself!

WILLIAM DAILEY

Owner of Dailey's Rare Books, appraiser of the Leary archives

Timothy Leary was the only person I have known to actively take part in his own demise. Most of us resign ourselves to watching death approach and, whether out of fear or in passivity, abandon what is left of life. Tim welcomed death, and as he had greeted the other big transitions of his life, he entertained the inevitable with active interest.

Even when his body began to die, his expansive spirit and curiosity remained courageously alert. In the last weeks some fear seeped through the drama, and while I wondered about his openness to that most natural and expected emotion, I cannot but be inspired by his creative departure.

RAM DASS

Spiritual teacher, original partner of Tim Leary in psychedelic research

Lesson: Tim demonstrated a balance of use of chemicals to reduce pain, enhance consciousness, and have fun. His salon was an extraordinary gift to allow his friends to share this event with him.

Favorite Memory: Looking for long periods into his eyes and seeing no one looking back, seeing how far back he was behind/beyond his theater piece of dying.

TOM DAVIS AND MIMI RALEIGH

Tom Davis is a comedian, writer, and host of Trailer Park *on the Sci Fi Network.*

Mimi Raleigh says that D.V.M. says it all.

Lesson: Tim was one of the most chronically happy people we have ever known, despite the fact that he was no stranger to tragedy. Somewhere in the middle of his dying process when we were there for a visit, we had a conversation about whether happiness was perhaps a gene with which Tim was most handsomely endowed. He agreed that it probably was.

Tom's Favorite Memory of Tim's Death: Tim and I were discussing the stigma from the use of cocaine, and I reminded him of the time a year before when we were in his favorite restaurant in Beverly Hills. When he asked me if I still had some cocaine left, I admitted that, yes, indeed, I did. Tim said "Well dump it on to the table—let everyone see! Drugs should be done in the open!"

I resisted Tim's attractive impulse and refused—wisely. But several weeks after, as I recalled the incident for him, he said, "Really? *I* said that? Oh . . . "

MICHELE EVANS

Member, Visiting Nurse Association, Yvette Luque Hospice

Lesson: The lesson that most strikes me about Tim's dying was that no matter how much we may talk about our lack of fear of dying or how we look forward to the journey, we all still experience fear when the time comes and find that the journey is much harder than we imagined. Tim learned this lesson and I learned it a little more than I had in my previous twelve years of doing hospice.

Favorite Memory: My favorite memory of Tim was one

day when I came to visit and his little granddaughter was visiting. I had to change a dressing on his leg and she was trying to be my helper. She tickled Tim's toes and he pretended to squeal in delight. The interaction between them was so real and so touching and so full of human emotion, I felt like I got a glimpse of Tim that he didn't often show to the world.

CAROLYN FERRIS

Visual artist, art director for Leary's Chaos and Cyberculture

Lesson: Through personal action, reaction, and interaction, we can make an art out of both living and dying.

Favorite Memory: I remember sitting with Tim in his study when his ever-so-intense blue eyes zeroed point-blank into my psyche—which always told me I'd better pay attention because an A+ response was expected. We were on our third glass of generic white wine (served from an expensive Merlot-labeled bottle into which it had been *accidentally* poured). I felt certain I was ready for his intelligence-bullet.

"I've got cancer," he said. "It's in an advanced stage." After a short pause: "It's okay."

I looked into those eyes, which filled slightly with water, as did mine. I could not speak. I hugged him, thinking that somehow he would beat this cancer thing like he had survived all of his lives within this one. He always pushed life to the limit by experiencing every second as if it was the most important.

The doorbell rang. I was still in shock when I returned to his study to announce the guest, but Tim was already back to his highly animated, upbeat self, entirely ready for the next minute's scenario.

There would never be the possibility of forgetting Tim.

ROBERT FORTE

Psychedelic expert, writer, editor of an upcoming collection of writings about Tim Leary

Favorite Memory: I'll never forget that St. Patrick's Day weekend, 1996. A Harvard reunion and Irish wake. There was a moment that Saturday afternoon when we were all—about thirty of us—in semicircles around the old boy in his wheelchair conducting, while we sang Irish folk songs. Tim was dapper, elfin, serene, mischievous, noble, dignified, happy. He was sparkling, lucid, brilliant, and dying. I didn't know it could be so beautiful. His ashen skin stretched tight against his fine, high cheekbones. His scruffy white beard. His body emaciated, twisted, and pained. His blue eyes had turned gray, yet he'd never felt better, he said glowing. "I'm just warning you. I've never felt better." There was a moment that St. Patty's Day, a break in ordinary reality, a numinous moment, when the magnificence of this rascal's life shone for all to see. I'll never forget that memory.

But it is no more my favorite than the memory of the following weekend, early Sunday evening, when there were a dozen friends, or more, crowded in his room sitting with him on his bed. There was a doctor, an old acid shrink, an actor, a producer, a director, beautiful men and women, his lawyer, a physicist, an L.A. Dodger and his gorgeous wife, and a seven-year-old boy sitting on the floor tossing a balloon around. Tim was engaging everyone in several conversations at once, all light, all funny. His attention flowed freely, with equal passion, dispassion, and mirth, to its object, whether it was a memory of his prison escape, a philosophical conjecture, or the balloon making its rounds.

Or maybe my favorite memory is spending time alone with him sorting through his archives, boxes of virtually every shred of paper that passed through his life. His archives are a cultural and historical treasure, the significance of which, clearly, is yet to dawn on modern society. For weeks, I read through those papers looking for mementos for his forthcoming memorial volume. The man kept everything: letters from his loving mother when he was at West Point (one, written to him when he was embroiled in a scandal there that threatened him with expulsion, was encouraging: "Don't worry dear son," she wrote. "If you don't make it through this it is because the Blessed Lord has something in store for you, perhaps something better"), hearing aid receipts, first psychedelic reports, love letters from his secretary, not-so-loving letters from Sandoz and the Harvard administration chastising him for excess publicity, even-less-loving CIA memos tracking him across Europe when he was in exile there, a fugitive. When I'd find something especially juicy I'd pull it out, show it to him, and he'd reminisce. I won't forget the childlike surprise and the glee that came from him as he exclaimed, "I can't believe what we did!"

But these memories are not complete without an account of the pain and terror he embraced as well in those final days . . .

BARBARA FOUCH AND JOHN ROSEBORO

Barbara Fouch is owner of Fouch-Roseboro, a public relations firm in L.A., and was a civils-rights activist in the sixties.

John Roseboro is a former L.A. Dodger catcher and civil rights activist in the 1960s.

Lesson: My husband, John Roseboro, and I join the many of Timothy's friends who spent time with and around him during his process of dying and who acknowledge the witnessing of a man who definitely "took charge" of the manner in which he was to die. To wit, he made a believer out of us!

Many people, when initially learning that they have a terminal illness, make claims similar to those made by Timothy. However, when approaching the final stages of their deaths, they express dread and resort to any and all means available to stave off the "grim reapers." Not Timothy!

Quite frankly, when Timothy understandably threw out of his home the representatives of the cryonics organization with which he had planned to have his head frozen (his reason being that they had become so bureaucratic he did not wish to return from death only to be greeted by people walking around with clipboards), I questioned whether he would deviate from some other of his philosophies of—and plans for—his final demise. However, this was not the case.

My husband accompanied Timothy to his various doctors on numerous occasions throughout his treatment stages. According to John, never once did Timothy express any fear of dying. I was with him constantly during this time and, specifically, several nights before his death, and I concur with John. Timothy, in my opinion, not only did not fear death, he was highly curious to learn whatever was awaiting him on the "other side."

Referring to his illness as "Mademoiselle Cancer," he played with her as she did him and, between periods of severe pain, he squeezed in more learning, living, sheer fun, and activity than do most people in a lifetime.

Having come from a large family in which there have been many deaths and funerals, I was truly amazed to be around someone who approached death so fearlessly.

As a result of these unique experiences with Timothy, death, for me, is no longer that "fearful journey into the deep, dark unknown," but a feeling of a question of "What's next?"

Conclusively, my husband and I feel honored to have known someone who, to the very end, did not fear death but, instead, focused on whatever was to be the next stage. We currently have several members of our families who are terminally ill, and Timothy's approach to death has provided my husband and me with a new level of acceptance and peace.

Favorite Memory: Our favorite memory of Timothy during the time of his illness stems from an outing at a Los Angeles Dodgers baseball game that Timothy, his beloved (then) ten-year-old granddaughter Sarah, my god-daughter Alexandra, John, and I attended. Timothy, a true baseball fan, was quite excited because John (a former Dodger catcher) was going to take Timothy down into the dugout to meet manager Tommy Lasorda as well as the players.

Our plans called for Timothy and Sarah to meet us at the stadium at 7:30 P.M. Extremely unusual for Timothy, he and Sarah were late . . . so late that, after numerous phone calls to his home, we started to become concerned. Just as we were preparing to leave the stadium to go to his home, we noticed a huge AAA auto repair truck pulling into the private Dodger Stadium parking lot. Out stepped Timothy and Sarah, who proceeded to run excitedly toward us. We all noticed that Timothy was waving a jacket that was smoldering with smoke and sporadic signs of fire. Timothy and Sarah seemed totally oblivious to this.

"My God, Timothy," I said. "What happened?" Timothy explained that his car had broken down and caught fire on the freeway while en route to meet us. As he removed his jacket and attempted to put out the fire, a Timothy Leary fan happened to pass by, recognized him, and stopped to help. They called AAA.

When the AAA truck arrived, Timothy promptly told the driver, "To hell with the car, get us to Dodger Stadium as quickly as possible." The driver tried to explain to Timothy that he could not solve the problem with his car unless he, the owner, remained with the car. Timothy simply grabbed Sarah and jumped into the AAA truck, told the fan to do whatever he wanted with his car, and again demanded that the driver get them to Dodger Stadium.

When we expressed concern about his car, he looked at us in disbelief and stated, "Are you guys crazy? You can always get another car but how many times can you take advantage of an invitation from Johnny Roseboro to be a guest in the Dodger dugout? Life is all about priorities, Kiddos." I'll never forget the joy that was registered on his face. He was like a little boy who was attending his very first baseball game.

Fortunately, as we were taking Timothy and Sarah home after the game, we returned to the site of the car and found it safely positioned on the side of the freeway. The next day, the car was repaired and returned home.

Timothy clearly had his priorities in order and not a day passes that we do not miss him helping us to keep ours the same.

AILEEN GETTY
Friend, artist

Favorite Memory: God how I miss him. My favorite memory took place five days before Tim soared elsewhere. I was spending the night with him and as night crept on and his guest bored him, he asked me to come to bed with him. As he sat on the side of the bed, birthing a pregnant balloon, I changed in his bathroom. I slipped on, with the same assurance as a broad from the forties, . . . a sheer gown, put a light shade of auburn on my lips, and perfume. I had never acted out this routine before in my life, but with the perfume scenting both sides of my neck, I stood up straight, shoulders lifting the air above, and walked slowly, wantonly down toward Timmy's bedroom. Timmy was elated, smiling as he repeated that I was his beauty. He asked me to turn around twice; I did, taking the time for Tim to see through my gown. "My beauty, come here." I sat on our bed, the bed where we spent an evening commemorating, with coloured Sharpies, our commitment as married souls and partners yet to discover, uncover, and rejoice in other worlds, worlds that had yet to be uncovered, discovered, and hover elsewhere. Timmy held me tightly, wandering within me. We kissed, both shaking, and Timmy quickly kissed me a couple more times as he ran his cold and trembling hands on my stomach and breasts, speaking of my beauty and his love for me. I felt him waning, tucked him in, switched off the light beside him, and crawled in beside him. Just before falling asleep, he asked me if my judge friend could marry us the next day. Absolutely, my Timmy. I listened to him breathe all night, frightened that he would stop.

NINA GRABOI

Artist; writer; director of the League for Spiritual Discovery Center in New York, 1966–68; director of the Third Force Lecture Bureau (late 1960s); "den mother" to the Flower Children in the 1960s; cosmic traveler

In Timothy's last months, two unfamiliar aspects of his personality came to the fore. One was a tenderness that made him seem like a little boy. The other was the grouchiness that is often associated with old men. I got a taste of both. His cadaverous body brought out the Jewish mother in me and made me urge him to eat—which infuriated him and brought out the grouchy old man. One day, after finishing his lunch, he turned to me with a broad grin. "See? I ate it all!" he said. "Kiss it!" he demanded, pointing to the top of his head. It was the sweet, innocent gesture of a little boy.

The show Timothy Leary put on in the 1960s was a holy mess. It was holy, and it poked holes into human consciousness, letting in some light. All over the world, thanks to Timothy Leary, little lights were kindled by a glance behind the veil through the holy holes poked by LSD.

Tim taught a generation to break away from outworn molds, to expand their minds; but his greatest teaching was his reinvention of the dying process. He was determined to break down the taboos that keep us from living fully. The process of dying is a taboo subject in our culture—a tragedy, something to be talked about in hushed tones, something abnormal and very sad. But death is normal, and Tim saw the humor in our traditional attitude toward dying. He approached his death with the same gusto he had lived his life. His dying show was the greatest show on earth.

CAMELLA GRACE

Founding member of Retina Logic, member of the Timothy Leary Homepage group

Sweet precious man. Authentic hero. Fearless prankster. I am one of the lucky ones to have known Tim intimately. There are moments in life when we touch the sensation of greatness. We are able to actualize in a breath a vision of grand potential. Tim was a great leader of people in the ride toward ecstasy. Reflecting on Tim's death, I see the profound chasm when such a strong life yields to the great unknown. What I learned from Tim at this time of his death was how to live.

Tim had an amazing ability in communicating to people's "higher" or better selves. He was a man who touched the future, studied the past, and sculpted the present. He was a master at living in the now, conducting an orchestra of the senses so there is no place for fear, ego, triviality and the only place left is to move . . . forward. His courage to be a futurist was in direct relation to mastering this poetic response to life. Rise to the occasion of being great! Do it fearlessly and joyously! He did this even in the face of death.

Most of us in this county are by-products of isolationism from a death-fearing culture. We consume and breed with the intention of finding an abstract greener pasture in some homogenized virtual shopping center with better packaging and less pain. Tim knew that there was no better place to live than by sharing your dreams, imagination, and vision with other people. He was a stubborn individualist who expected the same from everyone. He was tireless in his belief that we, as a social species, should work together, play together, live together, and die together.

He brought in a diverse group of people to rally his departure and made it work. I guess that is what he is famous for in his living and in his dying. Many times I watched Timothy actively and mischievously pulling people out of their self-obsessed worlds while fitting them with a new pair of perceptual trousers and then taking them out of the closet to play with counterperspectives. He changed my life every day that I was with him.

We had fun, Dr. Leary. Stricken with one of the most painful types of cancer, Tim never backed down from an adventure or the opportunity to work. He easily had ten of us working full time on new projects, new visions, new ways to explore the region of good living. Sense, sensualist, light. How do you say good-bye to this life? Very passionately, eating every moment as if it is the greatest food you have ever tasted. And by instilling the sense of the grand continuum, not in any spiritual sense but in life itself. He was always telling stories about his life only for each one of us to take the torch.

We watched Tim begin to leave his body so naturally. In his last few weeks, he become more preoccupied with the ethereal self. He spent a lot of time outside looking at the trees and the sky. I remember sitting on the lawn with him about a week and a half before he died. We were looking at his house in the sunlight. He was kind of rambling on about the lack of balance in the white house with the lawn furniture, but then he said, "White Light. If you could see what I see, what I see when I close my eyes, you would see White Light."

How do you say good-bye to such a beautiful soul who occupied so much space and gave so much to the world? I cannot listen to music, read a book, look at light without thinking of Tim or without asking: How can I live this moment more richly? Knowing him and loving him only makes me want to be a better person. I believe he infected thousands with the same purpose. If anyone of us can give one one-hundredth of what Tim gave to this world, we can say as he did, "I did a good job."

JAMES GRAUERHOLZ
Longtime personal assistant of William S. Burroughs

Lesson: Timothy approached the "problem" of dying exactly as he approached the "problem" of living: with flamboyance, self-promotion, and above all courage. I was relieved that, in the end, he did not carry out his announced online suicide, which I—in my conventionality?—found an appalling prospect. I received several eyewitness accounts of his last days and hours, and I am grateful for the example of bravery, calm, and acceptance that he gave us all.

Favorite Memory: My favorite memory of Tim in his last year is from the fall of 1995, when I arrived at LAX (for the mastering sessions of the *Naked Lunch* audiobook for Time Warner) with no hotel reservations. I called Tim from the car-rental agency at the airport, about 10:30 P.M., just to say hi. He immediately invited me to come right over and stay at his house for my four-day visit—a generosity of spirit that was utterly typical of Tim.

Although I was out of the house for long periods in the daytime, there was one night when he and I and a couple of friends sat at dinner at home, reminiscing about the many great times Tim and William Burroughs and I had spent together over the years since I first met him in 1978 as one of my guests at the first Nova Convention. Tim's memory was affected by his illness, so I was the one bringing up the experiences we'd shared—but when reminded, he remembered them well, and together we enjoyed an affirmation of our adventures in this lifetime. I miss him, I wish his spirit well, and I love him still.

ANITA HOFFMAN

Yippie! cofounder, ex-wife of Abbie Hoffman

Suddenly it was time to explore the death adventure and so he did, with humor, fortitude, curiosity, and full media coverage. But no matter how much he was quoted in the press about death, he continued to remind me always of life and laughter.

CINDY HOROWITZ

Video artist, longtime friend

Lesson: The most obvious lesson was that one pretty much dies the way one lives, if you're lucky enough to have an illness or circumstance that makes dying a conscious process. Tim loved people and communicating and had that uncanny Irish capacity—he was always the last to sleep, living or dying! And he anticipated everyone's curiosity about his process, embraced death with a kind of cavalier, high humor, and delighted in sharing his ups and downs. He broke many taboos and it was a gift.

Favorite Memory: My favorite memory happened in the week between Christmas and New Year 1996. Tim was still walking about and very happy to have all his grandchildren, family, and good friends around. He knew it was his last Christmas. People were stopping by constantly but it was early evening and a small group of us were hanging out in the living room. We'd been drinking a little wine and smoking a little grass and we started talking about our grandparents. Tim and I shared the good fortune of having grown up with ours and shared a slew of memories. We both felt charged by the recognition of their impact on us and that commonality.

MICHAEL HOROWITZ

Manager of the Leary archives, owner of Flashback Books

Lesson: That dying could be a work of performance art, a bravura adventure, a delightful farce, an occasion for entertaining your friends.

Favorite Memory: Timothy greeting me with "Get us each a balloon" (i.e., fill two balloons from the nitrous oxide tank), tapping our balloons as if clicking wine glasses, inhaling the laughing gas vapors while lying together in his bed, and then discussing postdeath linkup possibilities while gently floating back to our bodies.

LAURA HUXLEY

Writer, widow of Aldous Huxley

Lesson: The dying process is mysterious, solitary, personal—not to be judged.

Favorite Memory: Tim and I were always friends—but during the last few months he was more caring, more considerate and affectionate—it seemed to me that he had a greater need and appreciation for giving and receiving love.

PAUL KRASSNER

Yippie! cofounder, editor of The Realist, *stand-up comic*

Lesson: Tim died as he lived—participating fully in the process—with courage, wit, curiosity, generosity, propaganda, creativity, and, yes, especially pleasure. He didn't believe in an afterlife, so he extracted the juice out of every single mysterious moment on earth. Therefore, the lesson of his death was the lesson of his life, to have as much fun as possible, to be in control of that fun, to communicate that sense of fun to others, and to be responsible to it himself.

Favorite Memory: I asked him what he wanted his epitaph to be. Naturally he turned my question around and asked me to write his epitaph. I said, "Here lies Timothy Leary, a pioneer of inner space, and an Irish leprechaun to the end." He replied, "What is this Irish leprechaun shit? That's racist! Why can't there be a Jewish leprechaun?" "Okay," I said, "here lies Timothy Leary, a pioneer of inner space, and a Jewish leprechaun to the end." And then, during our final embrace, we laughed. I continue to be inspired by the way Tim didn't take himself as seriously as he took his journey.

RON LAWRENCE

Independent Macintosh consultant, musician, filmmaker; Timothy's friend and Macintosh tutor, mentor, assistant, and personal handyman

Lesson: The lesson for me of Tim's performance of the dying experience is to live every day consciously, to cherish every moment because, ready or not, it's over. And you don't have to die alone. Physician-assisted suicide is the wrong question. But home palliative care is the answer.

Favorite Memory: My favorite memory from that time was the night he proved that attempts to create distance between us were unsuccessful by taking hold of my lapel, pulling my face down to his face, and saying, "Ronnie, I love you very much."

ROSEMARY WOODRUFF LEARY

Wife and partner of Timothy Leary during the great 1960s adventure and 1970s exile, trustee of the Leary Foundation

Lesson: Tim upleveled dying to a state of loving art. He achieved a consciousness that allowed his heart to match his ego and intellect. I learned to be in love again with the life we had shared.

Favorite Memory: That, in the last adventure of this life, we were again able to speak silently, heart to heart.

ZACH LEARY

Stepson via Tim Leary's last wife, Barbara; member of the Timothy Leary Homepage group

Lesson: When you're young, death doesn't take on any shape or form. It's hard to make sense of it. During the last three months of Tim's life, I had the hardest time putting my finger on what the end was supposed to look like. To be honest, I thought there would be no end, perhaps just a winding, endless road of deterioration and other physical complications. What led me to believe all this was Timmy's endless supply of bravery and courage. He treated the endless sleep with great intensity and admiration. I was more scared than he was. He taught me that one of the greatest, most profound mysteries of life does indeed come at that "three to fifteen minutes" when breathing has stopped and the brain is gearing up for the ultimate.

We need not die in a hospital surrounded by AMA doctors who are spending thousands to keep you holding on; we must let go and enjoy the adventure. Tim had the sensitivity to share this with us. He wanted us to understand that it *was* okay for him to leave us. He knew it would have pained us all to see him die in a controlled setting with wires and do-dads attached to his body. Designer Dying is now one of the quintessential blueprints he left to a confused Western culture. I hope we all can share the lesson for generations to come.

Favorite Memory: My favorite memory during crunch time were the "sneak peeks." On any given afternoon or evening, Tim would nod off into never-never land, only to return with a look of loving bewilderment. He once said, "If you could see what I see when I close my eyes, brilliant white light! A sneak preview!"

This to me was so shocking, I couldn't believe what he was going through. In spite of this natural drama, he kept his sense of humor. His inherent need to keep us happy while teaching us something is my fondest memory. Even in dire straits, his circus kept us entertained.

MICHAEL LEONARD

Co-owner of Wireless Multi-Media in the San Francisco area, researcher of Timothy's life for a CD-ROM biography project

Lesson: Before I met Tim, dying seemed terrifying, tragic, and mysterious in a remote, inaccessible way. While the process of watching Tim die still has lingering sadness, the fear has subsided. My associations with death are now those of a man surrounded by loved ones, ending a life completely and well lived with a wry, mischievous smile.

Favorite Memory: My favorite memory is of Tim, at Wavy Gravy's Hog Farm, standing on top of Ken Kesey's bus with a wizard's hat and a sorcerer's cape, shouting "Get on the bus!"

JOHN LILLY

Intrepid psychonaut, author, legend

Lesson: His insight and courageous facing of transiting to beyond the biophysical realities.

Favorite Memory: His happiness in moving toward his own future.

AREL LUCAS

Friend, cryonics advocate

Lesson: The lesson for me was that planning for this process can be very difficult and may be impossible, since who one is at that point may not be foreseeable. Perhaps reminders to oneself why one set up things the way one did might be useful.

Favorite Memory: My favorite memory is of a visit in Timothy's bedroom, when he stood up carefully and with obvious difficulty but with deliberation, slowly opened his arms wide, and hugged me. His manner bespoke a considered and considerate effort to fashion a memory of that moment for me. It worked.

VICKI MARSHALL

Writer; editor; co-owner of a small Macintosh consulting and desktop publishing company called KnoWare, which published "Timothy Leary's Greatest Hits, Vol. 1" in 1990 and makes Leary publications available by mail order; creator of Timothy's "Just Say KNOW" campaign; Timothy's editor, collaborator, archivist, Macintosh wizard, office manager, administrative coordinator, personal assistant, and primary health-care coordinator; currently administrative coordinator for the Leary Estate and Futique Trust

Lesson: The lessons for me of Tim's performance of the dying process are multilevel:

- That death isn't something that "happens to you"; it's the last act of the performance of life and we have the right to perform it in our own individual style.

  To do it with friends, do it with friends, do it with friends.

  That cultural taboos about death are steeped in and perpetuate the fear and denial that alienate the dying from their loved ones. And vice versa.

  That one of the hardest things about dying is letting go of life.
- That Home Hospice makes all the difference in caring for the star performer, the supporting cast, and crew.

That radiation treatments sometimes do more harm than good.

That most physicians are more in denial about death than their terminal patients. They routinely fail to provide or prescribe pain relief, and their seeming disregard for their patient's well-being is abominable. (Don't get me started.)

That operating a manually driven wheelchair takes considerable practice, skill, and upper-body strength. And navigating one on carpeted floors is like trying to drive it through snow.

That it's tough to put socks on somebody else's feet.

That there are subtle but noticeable changes in appearance once the brain's deanimation circuits become activated.

That a Duragesic patch beats the hell out of MS Contin tablets for pain management.

- That I'm awesome in a crisis.
- That there IS a light at the end of the tunnel.
- That I'm not nearly finished processing the lessons of Timothy's performance of the dying process.

Favorite Memory: Helping him shower, bundling him up in towels, getting him dressed, and especially brushing his hair for him. I then wheeled him out to the other room where attorneys were waiting to take his deposition. The proceedings got under way and I was excused, only to repeatedly be called in to serve as Tim's memory since his was failing and mine is renowned. Finally Tim asked that I be permitted to sit beside him and the attorneys agreed. Their first question to me was how long I'd been working with Tim. I answered, "About ten years." Tim turned to me and said, "No, you've been with me much longer than that." Our eyes met and engaged in an eternal, nonverbal exchange. After which he became very emotional and started to cry.

And the night I sat beside Tim on his bed and told him that my mind was giving me "dress rehearsals" of his death in my dreams. He leaned his head on mine and said, "Me too."

Please include the following . . .

HOME HOSPICE

by Vicki Marshall

Hospice care. The mere mention fills many with fear and dread. Much of this comes from modern culture's prevailing tendency to deny our mortality. But sooner or later we must all exit this mortal coil. And that's why we should all know about Home Hospice.

I was assistant to—and administrative coordinator for—the late Dr. Timothy Leary. Dr. Leary was diagnosed with terminal prostate cancer in January 1995. By December his cancer had metastasized to the bones in his lower back. He was losing mobility and was in increasingly severe pain.

His doctors were reluctant to prescribe adequate pain medication. Inadequate pain management is a common practice, despite numerous articles in the *Journal of the American Medical Association* about the negative repercussions on patients' health and recovery.

When a bone scan confirmed what Tim already knew, his doctors recommended three weeks of radiation therapy. They said the radiation would decrease the size of the tumor, which would relieve the pressure on his spine. They predicted he'd be feeling better by the end of the second week.

He didn't. In fact, by the middle of the second week, he felt worse. And he looked terrible. Alarmed by his rapid deterioration, I called his doctors and was told he should complete the radiation treatments. They reluctantly wrote prescriptions for mild analgesics.

By the third week, Timothy was in excruciating pain and could no longer walk. Always fiercely independent, cheerful, and healthy, he became increasingly dependent, depressed, and demanding. We rented a wheelchair for him from a medical supply house and managed to persuade his doctor to sign the necessary papers so it would be covered by Medicare.

Timothy Leary wasn't just my employer, he was my friend. It's hard to watch someone you love be ravaged by cancer, weakened by radiation treatments, and denied adequate pain medication. I could no longer find it within myself to encourage him to continue with the radiation treatments.

I was at my wit's end when I received email from a mutual friend (who was also handling the paperwork for Timothy's cryonic preservation) asking how things were. In desperation, I told her everything about Timothy's deteriorating condition. She forwarded my reply to a colleague who forwarded it to Dr. David Crippen of the St. Francis Medical Center, Department of Critical Care Medicine in

Pittsburgh, Pennsylvania. Dr. Crippen, in turn, called the Visiting Nurses of Los Angeles' Home Hospice Program.

Hospice arrived the following day in the form of Michele Evans and Jackie Garbarino.

They were kind, soft-spoken, incredibly considerate, and very competent. They assessed Timothy's condition and instantly began a regime of pain management. I trusted them immediately.

In the weeks that followed, I learned that Hospice care is only provided for terminal patients with six months or less to live. The VNA-LA Home Hospice Program is designed to provide support and care for the terminally ill person and his or her family. They know the terminally ill cannot effect the necessary closure in their lives while they're in severe pain, so they focus on the control of pain and other symptoms of the illness to make the remaining time as comfortable and meaningful as possible.

This made a world of difference in Timothy's last three months.

Hospice provided everything we needed from medications to hospital beds. They gave us access to their medical director, registered nurses, home health aids, bath attendants, coordinators, nutritional consultants, social workers, pharmacists, physical therapists, spiritual counselors, and volunteers.

Home hospice meant no more torturous visits to doctor's offices, no more supplicant pleading for pain relief, no more pain-induced insomnia. It also meant less stress, frustration, and worry for us. The visiting nurses always made time to answer our questions and listen to our concerns. They taught us how to care for Timothy and gave us counseling and support during his illness. They even offered continued support and bereavement counseling for the period following his death.

The Home Hospice Program took the suffering out of the dying process. Within a week of their arrival, Timothy's depression lifted and his quality of life improved. He resumed active participation in ongoing projects, he visited with longtime friends, he went out on the town. Many times. There were times when he truly believed he was getting better.

And in a way, he was. Not physically, but mentally, emotionally, psychologically. When the end drew near, he was prepared. And so were we.

Timothy Leary died peacefully in the comfortable and familiar surroundings of his home on Friday, May 31, 1996, surrounded by friends and loved ones.

And a Hospice volunteer.

RALPH METZNER

Author, teacher, therapist, original partner of Tim Leary in psychedelic research

Lesson: Timothy was a storyteller and teacher in the Native American tradition of Coyote the Trickster and, like that laughing philosopher, often fell victim to his own inspired pranks. However, his most masterful teaching concerned the process of dying. Having been marginalized all his life for his outrageous views on drugs, or space, or computers, or reality, he had the full attention of the media when he declared, in all seriousness, that he was going to plan dying to be like a psychedelic session with careful attention to set and setting and to be a joyous adventure. He was not kidding . . . and in accordance with his lifelong teaching, he took control of his own dying process.

Favorite Memory: In my last visits with him, I found him to be physically frail but mentally as sharp and present as ever. He had lost none of his capacity to give his full appreciative attention to someone, and his wit and laughter was infectious, as always.

CHARLES PLATT

Author, cryonics advocate, frequent Wired *contributor*

Lesson: Many separate thoughts occur to me. He was the toughest, most rebellious man. For many weeks he seemed to feel his willpower could postpone death. To some extent, he may have been right—but only to some extent. His bravado in the face of pain was amazing to watch. It was also distressing, because it denied reality. Ultimately, disease processes were more powerful than life processes. Willpower alone is not the best weapon against death.

CAROL ROSIN

Space advocate, activist against militarization of space, coordinator of the mission to place Leary's ashes into orbit

Lesson: I learned from Tim's performance of the dying process that it was just that, a performance. It was not the only reality of his dying process. He was teaching us that we are the light, that we have many realities to experience, and about love and light, and that we are free to choose.

Timothy's life was full of contradictions and inconsistencies; his dying performance was too. In other words, Timothy clearly enjoyed his own dying performance, making his audience feel dying was what he wanted to do, that dying was a fun process that could be done with enthusiasm with friends around. With the curtain up, he was the ultimate teacher he loved to be. Yet in another reality he was experiencing a lot of suffering, fear, anger, depression, and sadness that he didn't let most people see.

I spent all night with him most of the last nights of the last months of his life. I never left his side during those nights. After everyone left, the curtain fell. In the "dressing room," it was different. We were alone.

He requested my presence, he said, because I was the only friend he had who didn't listen to anything he said. As his time came closer and things became more difficult for him, and for me, I began to understand why he wanted me there. He didn't want to sleep, which I expected was natural. I thought it was natural that he didn't want to waste a minute sleeping. I could see he wanted to spend time every night reviewing his life. That was the easy part, and a valued pleasure. He showed me his writings, videotapes, letters, photographs, etc. He was so proud of his achievements and experiences, and I felt honored to be there.

I was always exhausted but the real strain during those lonely nights was when his physical and emotional pain became excruciating, when he shook with fear and sobbed with regrets and loneliness, when I had to hold him down to calm him down, and hold him up to clean him up in the shower from what became a great embarrassment to him. He became nasty, hateful (more than usual). But while there were moments when I wondered why I would stay, I didn't listen.

He'd thank me for not walking out. I saw how difficult dying was for him. How difficult it was to pull himself together to perform for people as they arrived and visited during the long days and evenings. The ultimate actor/producer—the show would go on—and did, to his last breath.

He didn't want me to leave him alone at night. On occasions, when I would leave to check in on my house and life, he'd call me to come back immediately. On one particular night, I thought he'd be happy that another woman friend would spend the night with him (we couldn't leave him unattended). He became furious with me for allowing this woman to stay all night. Although she hadn't known him for more than a few short months, she presumed it was okay to crawl into bed next to him to keep him company.

Although he seemed to be fine around her, I learned even that was a performance. He didn't want her there. Oh, he acted as though he did when she was around. Once, he tried to sit up in his wheelchair all night because he was afraid of being seen at his worst.

Sometimes, Timothy performed as though he wanted crowds. Sometimes he pretended he wanted to go out to restaurants, but really he wanted to stay home and have dinner delivered. He was tired. He didn't want anyone to know. Toward the end, he wanted only a few close people around him. He was happy much of the time, especially when his mind was occupied and when loving friends communicated. Even when in extraordinary pain or drugged in order to dull the pain, he performed well when people came to see him or called.

The parties gradually ended. And, eventually, he couldn't keep up with his own script. He couldn't remember the lines, sometimes the names of friends. Still, he loved any kind of publicity and would do almost any kind of performance to get it. In fact, Web-wise, on that last day, I believe he would have loved to perform his death live, but that performance never happened.

He loved public relations, interviews and such, especially now, as this was to be his farewell performance about his death and dying process. I did the very last interview with him on videotape. In it, he talked about how we are the light—light is who we are, he said, and our purpose is to shine that light on others. He talked about how he loved Celestis, the Houston-based company that arranged the launch of his ashes into space, because, he said, they have "set us free to ride the light into space with our friends."

Yes, Timothy gave the performance of his lifetime—portraying a man who was teaching that dying is/was/can be a joyful experience, that it is possible to choose how we live and die, with whom, and when. This show gave him the widest of ranges in which to develop his character, to show us all his intelligence, talent, skills, ego, and spirit. And his splendid courage!

What I saw was his performance messages, that in life and in death "you can be anyone this time around" and that we are "free to ride the light" on earth and into space. That life and death are about peace, love, and light. That we are one. That even in your dying process, you can be a happy person who enjoys the hummingbirds, who remembers the spiritual dimension of who we are. That we can track and make fun of the pain and the living/dying process. He showed us we can all perform almost anything, anytime.

But the best part of his performance occurred on the day he died. When he drove around outside in his backyard in the early morning in his electric wheelchair as though he was saying good-bye to the birds and trees he loved so much, when he climbed into bed to begin the slow breathing process that he knew would lead to his death, and when he periodically said a few words and smiled lovingly to all who surrounded him in that candlelit room, with that Leary sense of humor, during that long day and night until 12:04 A.M. when, with a few friends who sat by his side and others who awaited this moment in the living room, he finally got out of his body. He loved to perform. Now, his living performance became his dying performance, and I was so sad to know his show was over.

I was the most fortunate person in the world to have had my fingers on the artery in his neck when the pulse of Dr. Timothy Leary, my dear friend, faded and disappeared, when his final curtain went down.

Favorite Memory: My favorite memory is also my saddest memory of Timothy. He called me to come to him as he sat alone in his wheelchair. His head was slumped downward onto his chest. Just a few minutes before he had told me that he didn't recognize the thin, frail person in his mirror. But now, he had something more profound to say, something that hurt me deeply and made me see his vulnerability, his loneliness:

"You know what the saddest part of this whole thing is?" Timothy asked.

"What, Timothy?" I asked as softly as he was speaking.

"That I don't even have a wife."

DOUG RUSHKOFF

Author, media theorist

Lesson: "Performance" is an oddly appropriate word for Tim's death. A final show. At first, it was as if he didn't take his own death seriously. When he got the news of his terminal cancer he treated the whole thing as an opportunity—another taboo to be exposed and exploited. More provocative than drugs, more liberating than cyberspace: deanimation.

Once we got over how morbid it was, it turned into a great game. A celebration of life in the face of a process that's supposed to be so shameful and private. There were more parties—more good parties—at Tim's house than ever before. It was the happiest I had seen Tim since his marriage to Barbara. Death was just an excuse to enjoy life.

I thought that was destined to be the lesson. Go out gloriously. It was an approach to life that summed up almost all of Tim's work from personality through politics. Don't listen to what "they" say; do what you want to. Deprogram from the stigma and experience the joy. Taking back the right to die the way you want to is the ultimate example of taking back the right to live the way you want to.

Surprising Tim as much as anyone, the Designer Dying meme caught on bigger than any of us expected. Maybe it was Kevorkian, maybe it was the fact that so many baby boomers are watching their parents die these days, or maybe it had something to do with computers and consciousness. But the more people and TV shows that got interested in the death of Timothy Leary, the bigger that death would have to become.

That's how the videotaped death broadcast over the Internet idea got started. The deanimation chamber (his bedroom) would be the scene of the world's first televised death. Even his plans to freeze his brain were expanded to include a photo spread of the freezing process in a major magazine. TV crews visited the house daily, and Tim began to spend all his waking, conscious hours in the service of his meme. Tim was no longer dying for himself; he was dying for the rest of us—a prisoner of Designer Dying advocacy.

But Tim soon saw that to die the way he wanted to, and even as an example for the rest of us, he'd have to get rid of the aspects of this dying spectacle that he didn't enjoy. He canceled interviews, dropped the idea of the online death, canceled his freezing, and even began "banishing" people (usually strangers who had wandered in for predeath memorabilia or autographs) from the house who overly annoyed him.

He took a lot of criticism for backing out of his "original plan." But what these harsh critics didn't understand is that Timothy Leary's original plan was not to do a mediated death—it was to die exactly as he wanted to.

Well, Tim's exact vision of his dying moment evolved over time. For a while, he wanted the hypermediated death; then he changed his mind. If he had stayed tied to his original announcements, he might as well already been dead.

For me, the lesson of Tim's death is that as long as you're alive, you can live however the hell you want to; to give in to what people expect of you is to die before your time.

Favorite Memory: I used to find it funny that Tim would say the same things so often. For years, whenever he'd walk out onto his back patio high up in Beverly Hills, he'd look at the Los Angeles panorama and exclaim, "Isn't that beautiful?!" It was as if he were seeing it for the first time from the terrace of a hotel room.

A week or so before Tim died, he woke up early one morning and asked me to wheel him outside. We watched the sun come up. In silence he took in the scene. Then he broke the stillness to exclaim his usual "Isn't that beautiful?!" I nodded and maybe smiled or said yes.

Tim took my hand. I could feel the edges of the crusty bandages covering his bleeding sores. "This is a beautiful place," Tim reaffirmed. A delighted tourist.

URI RYDER

Actor, one of Leary's young friends

Lesson: That a person's contagious glee for being alive doesn't have to stop when he learns he's going to be terminated.

Favorite Memory: I have so many memories of my wild excursions up to the old Doctor's playground. One stands out in particular—a time I visited him on impulse after taking a hit of blotter.

Upon entering his bedroom I was told that the old man was being given a shot of ketamine. We nodded to one another, and he gestured toward his closet. Without hesitation I stepped around a band of freaks sitting on the floor, arriving at a nitrous oxide tank the size of a small human in his closet. Sometime later, after too many balloons on top of the acid, I found myself on the edge of Tim's bed staring at his carpet for what seemed like the rest of the millennium. His bedroom had filled up with people I didn't know and the thought of attempting conversation with any of them seemed impossible.

Feeling lost in the void, I looked over at Tim who himself seemed a bit uneasy by the sheer number of freaks and drug-induced chaos in his bedroom. Someone passed me yet another balloon. I was at first inclined to reject it, but I found myself muttering those now famous words, "Why not?" I sucked half of it down and passed in to the Doctor, who sucked down the rest. Then something glorious happened. It sends a shiver up my spine just thinking about it. The old Doc and I looked up at each other at the exact same time. Our eyes locked. Time seemed to stop. We became oblivious to all the chaos, and for what must have been thirty seconds but seemed much longer we peered into the depths of each other's souls. It left me with a feeling of incredible warmth that I carried with me for days afterward and still feel when I talk about it.

MICHAEL D. SEGEL
Friend, filmmaker

Lesson: I experienced several deaths in the same year that Timothy passed. Each friend and family member shared their own unique lessons with me, some directly, some less so. At thirty-eight, I had certainly experienced death before, but never with so many that I was so close to nor in such a condensed period of time. There were car accidents, two on subsequent days, long-term illnesses, and short-term illnesses. Some were too young, others well on in years. I saw each person go through the dying process in their own way. This was not a process divorced from the life that preceded it. How we died, it seemed to me, was a function of how we had lived.

Timothy carried out his performance of dying as singularly as his performance of living. He opened so many areas of exploration for me, through our friendship. His dying would be no different.

He told us that, when he was young it was said that you never discussed two things: how much money you made and death. Tim felt strongly that the dying process was something that should be shared with friends and discussed openly. This he did.

Timothy approached the dying process as simply another one of life's stages to be explored. This example proved to be a tremendous example to me. The decisions made here, he told us, were the most important in our lives.

He approached dying as a "work in progress" and constantly redefined how he would perform it. He continually reformed and recreated his models of death and dying. How he pursued the process in September was more than likely going to be different from how he pursued it in January. He would not be forced into any one determination. In answering each reporter's questions, and there were a multitude over the year, he reminded them that this was how he felt today—tomorrow he might feel differently. This seems an appropriate way to approach death. Hell, it seems an appropriate way to approach life.

At various times over Tim's last year, different aspects of the process seemed to intrigue him. Initially he seemed concerned with developing a method of determining the current quality of his life experience. To this end, he created a graph for charting his "quality of life" as his dying progressed. Because he believed that we should be allowed to determine the time of our own death, he needed a method of judging what was important to him and how he fared in each category on any given day.

The graph he created charted his estimation of the quality of his appearance, sense of humor, mobility, etc., by rating each category on a sliding scale from one (lowest) to six (highest). He told me that when he reached an average of two on the scale he would decide to end his life. He believed that each dying person should create their own chart by determining what was important to them and what their own minimum level of acceptability was.

Though ultimately he did not need to take an active role in ending his life, his process in determining what was important to him was a great lesson.

In 1987, I produced some shows with Timothy at Carlos and Charlie's on the Sunset Strip. Each show had a different guest: John Lilly, Robert Anton Wilson, Paul Krassner, and one evening the president of the cryonics company ALCOR. It seemed to me then that Timothy was as interested in posing basic philosophical questions to the audience as he was in the exploration of this new technology. "We are told that the only certainties in life are death and taxes. How does the possibility of the end of death as we know it influence your life? If, instead of dying, we go into periods of suspended animation followed by periods of reanimation, does that change the way you live your life? Is this something you desire?"

I was quite surprised to hear the audience response. Many became furious at the mere discussion of the possibility. "What happens to your soul? You're cheating God!" they shouted. "God needs your soul." "Not my god," responded

Timothy with his famous smile. "She wants me to be as creative as I can be with the life I've been given."

He admitted that, "It's a long shot. They don't yet know how to revive you and perhaps never will. The only thing that is a longer shot is planting yourself in the ground and letting the worms eat you." The audience's fury did not subside. Tim was giving people a chance to examine an absolute belief—that we all must die some day. The mere discussion had an alchemical quality to it. This, for Tim, was the game. He admitted to me later that he wasn't sure that he'd avail himself of this new technology.

I was there when he met with a couple of members of CryoCare last year, a group that had splintered off from another cryonics group, ALCOR. For quite a while Timothy wore ID bracelets from both groups. This infuriated representatives of each. In fact, though these seemed to me bright and committed pioneers, a more humorless bunch I have rarely seen. One of the chief researchers admitted to us that he didn't enjoy life and had no intention of using cryonic freezing himself. Instead, he was committed to developing the technology for those who did enjoy life.

In the end, I believe one of the primary reasons Tim did not go the way of liquid nitrogen was that CryoCare couldn't cotton to his public discussion of terminating his own life. These cryonics companies are nervous when confronted by legal complications, and quite rightly I suppose. They can't freeze you until you're clinically dead and then need to slip you into the liquid nitrogen as quickly as possible to limit any further cellular destruction. If the body is sent to a coroner because of the suspicion of suicide or homicide, the jig is up. They most certainly don't want to be accused of being a party to either.

It was in dealing with more traditional medicine that Timothy gave me one of my more pragmatic lessons. He became furious with me one morning for accepting on face value the latest proclamation of one of his doctors. He told me that my view of doctors as omnipotent was so ingrained that I couldn't even sense its existence. He was right. Many of us in the house tended to respond to doctors' warnings as if a declaration had been handed down from on high. Tim refused to let decisions about his health be taken away from him. This has already influenced my dealings with members of the medical profession.

When assessing his life's work, Timothy often said (and I paraphrase), "One-third of what I've said is commonplace, not interesting or innovative. Another third is just plain wrong. But the final third is world class, and if you bat .333 as your lifetime average, they put you in the Hall of Fame." That's where Timothy belongs. Right where he wanted to be. Voted MVP: Most Valuable Philosopher.

Favorite Memory: I spent much of Timothy's last year with him. Though I was working on a couple of films that year, I spent weekends and a few nights each week staying over at his house. My memories from that time are rich and numerous. They range from the seemingly commonplace (although no experience with Tim was ever truly commonplace) to the extraordinary. From jumping up to watch the national news and discuss the events of the day, to working with him on an article for an avant-garde Japanese magazine until three in the morning. There were visits from the dear friends and great minds who stopped by to spend time with Timothy and, later on, to say good-bye. There were quiet drives that he and I shared alone.

One such drive, longer than most, is permanently etched in my memory.

The adventure began with a phone call to Tim from O. B. Babbs, one of the sons of Ken Babbs, the famous Merry Prankster. O.B. was calling to reiterate an invitation Timothy had received from Ken Kesey and Ken Babbs. They had invited Timothy to go to the annual "Hog Farm Pignic [*sic*]" with them. The "Pignic" was Wavy Gravy's and the Hog Farm's weekend-long, tribal gathering in Laytonville, California.

I knew of the original invitation because I regularly read Tim's email with him. I offered to accompany Timothy on the trek. Initially the whole idea of the trip seemed too much for Tim. After all, his cancer was progressing. Nonetheless, I repeated my offer to accompany him if he decided to go.

On the Wednesday preceding the "Pignic" weekend, Timothy called. He had received an offer to speak in Chico, California, on that Sunday. It was to be one of Tim's last road trips and another chance for him to publicly explore the dying process.

The airport was crazed at eight o'clock that Friday morning. It was the beginning of Memorial Day weekend and LAX was packed. I found Timothy at the gate and though every flight was delayed, we managed to make it as far as San Francisco.

By the time we landed in San Francisco, we found that the flight to Sacramento had also been delayed but would be leaving in minutes. We began to run. The connecting gate, as seems to be the rule at airports, was in a different terminal. We arrived at the distant gate just as they were closing the door. I yelled to them to wait. They did and ushered us onto the small prop.

We had made it. This plane would take us to Sacramento and then, following a few local stops, on to Laytonville.

Or not.

When we arrived at the Sacramento airport, Timothy and I disembarked to grab a quick cigarette and cup of coffee. We then waited to reboard. Instead we were informed by an overworked ticket agent that they had overbooked the small plane. They wanted to fly us back to San Francisco where we would spend the night. There were no other flights available to Laytonville.

After much arguing, Timothy turned to me with a smile and suggested we rent a car and drive the rest of the way. I had already considered this option but was concerned that the long drive would be too much of a strain on my dying friend. He had no such concern.

We paged O.B. and his friend A.J., who were waiting for us at the airport in Laytonville. I told them of our change in travel plans and received directions to the tiny motel half an hour outside Laytonville, itself not exactly a bustling metropolis, where we would stay the night.

We went to rent a car. While choosing the car for the journey, I spotted a make I hadn't heard of before. It was called an Intrepid. I booked it immediately. After all, what an appropriately named vehicle for a meeting with the intrepid travelers themselves, the founders of Intrepid Trips, Ken Kesey, Ken Babbs, and the Merry Pranksters.

There began one of the great drives of my life. Timothy and I packed up the car, spun the radio dial until we found a great college rock 'n' roll station and took off.

The farther north we traveled, the more scenic the landscape became.

Timothy became thoughtful. He gave me his Timothy Leary northern California prison tour. He regaled me with stories from his life, meetings with great people, stories of ex-wives, and more.

We were re-creating a drive along Highway 40 that he had taken several times while incarcerated.

Seven hours later we arrived at the tiny motel. It was eleven o'clock at night. The bus "Further" had not yet arrived, having broken down several times on the trip south from Oregon. I was later told that Kesey, though he has great mechanical skills, would only repair the bus just enough to get it on the road again.

The following morning, Timothy met up with the two Kens for the first time in years.

After breakfast, we headed down the road for about a mile. We stopped to regroup and for Kesey to "debrief" us.

That's when Ken told us of his plan. We were to lash a chair to the top of the bus, sit Timothy on top of it, and drive him through the crowd at the gathering. Once parked, Ken's plan was to "cannonize" Timothy. By "cannonize" Ken meant that he was going to shoot off a very loud cannon from on top of the bus, directly next to Tim and me.

Once on the grounds of the gathering, they placed Timothy on his chair atop the bus. I sat in a beanbag chair next to him as a safety. "We're Coming to Take You Away" blasted from the speakers on the bus as we drove through the crowd. Timothy and the two Kens began a psychedelic rap that lasted until we finally stopped in front of the stage where Wavy Gravy chimed in. I will never forget the faces of the amazed crowd as they gawked at the painted bus and up at Timothy.

Ken spoke to the crowd, spouting his love and admiration for Timothy. Timothy then expressed the same for Ken. Timothy finished by shouting out to the crowd that he intended to "live every day as if were my last!"

Later the bus was parked off to the side and groups of people began stopping by. Timothy mentioned that there were a lot of people there, some very young, who already had smile wrinkles etched into their faces. "Only one way to get those," he said. "You can't order them from your plastic surgeon."

Tim also mentioned that there were one or two guys who looked an awful lot like Charlie Manson mingling in the crowd. At that moment, as if on cue, one of those fellows poked his head through the door of the bus and mumbled, "I've got a .38."

Adrenaline began pumping through my veins... until he added, "But it's got a '41 chassis." He was, of course, telling us that he had a 1938 International bus not unlike the Pranksters'. He smiled and headed back into the crowd.

The next day, Tim and I said our good-byes and drove another seven hours to the Chico nightclub where he was to speak that evening, Timothy telling more stories along the way. We finally arrived in Chico for a press conference that preceded the event by a couple of hours.

Timothy's energy level never waned. It was always hard to explain to people how difficult it was to keep up with this man who was twice my age and was "suffering" from cancer.

That night, Timothy spoke to the crowded room about his experience of the dying process. The response was incredible. Few had experienced such a public discussion of what was usually such a private event, let alone in a nightclub. Many came up to Tim afterward and told him just that.

The feeling in the room was electric. I have heard Timothy speak often over the years, but this night seemed different. The effect of Tim's discussion of dying was unmistakably cathartic for those in attendance.

The last thing I remember from that evening was sitting next to Timothy as he spotted a man in his forties escorting his elderly father around. It seems the old man was suffering from an extreme case of Alzheimer's. "Never let me get like that," he told me.

He never did. Timothy stayed sharp until the end. His memory did begin to "soften" over his last year, which he considered a very creative experience. He told me that he found himself making new conceptual connections, combinations his mind had not put together before. "Besides," he would say, "senility isn't so bad. I get to meet new and exciting people every day."

TRUDY TRUE(LOVE)

Booking/scheduling assistant for Tim Leary during the entire "Dying Performance," artist, musician

Lesson: During the four months I was employed by Timothy, I learned *so many* lessons in such a regrettably short period of time, it's hard to pinpoint the importance of one over another. I saw the whole picture at once: each brilliantly cut facet of Timothy's life gleaming into the next. As Tim's booking assistant, one of my duties was to help him orchestrate a chaotic media blitz about his death that got at times gruesome, tacky, and exploitative. Not always the more eloquent and dignified tribute I felt he deserved, but he loved *all of it*—the tabloids, the rumors, the glorious attention in whatever form. He appreciated it and had fun with it, but it was burning him out. He wanted to burn out like the brightest flame that consumes all it touches. This is what the public saw: one slight sliver of his expiring life, and this is what I saw as the "performance aspect of his dying experience," and it's the only thing we ever argued about. I thought it was a courageous thing to do, to present your dying moment in a public arena, and he had the healthiest attitude about dying of anyone I've ever met, but I didn't like other people's interpretation of the event. There was even a sort of bidding war going on for a few days when Timothy suggested to an AP reporter that he might commit suicide on the Web. It *was* grotesquely funny having people offer money for a public death, but I thought the guy was a genius, and—although I hated to see him in pain—I personally wanted to see him live as long as possible.

The most touching memories I have of Timothy were not involving the performance, but when the cameras were off. Then I felt like I was in the most honorable position of being his friend. I was able to comfort him and to witness the absolutely honest love that almost everyone around Timothy felt for him. To see a man so impressive in his achievements and so worldly receive his old friends in his last days was a legendary part of my life that will haunt me forever in the best possible ways. As enthusiastic as he may have seemed about dying, ultimately it really pissed Tim off that he had to leave the party! I'm still sorting it all out, but one of the main lessons I have learned from being a part of Timothy's dying experience is humility. I served the servant. I did his bidding and tried to keep him from pain, harm, and boredom. I had no motives other than to see him out gracefully. He earned it.

Favorite Memory: Other than the first night I met Timothy in his home, which was amazing and hilarious and whacked-out and crazy . . . I would have to say there was a particular night when Tim had some old friends over to visit, about two months or so before he died. We were watching a Canadian documentary about the "evils" of LSD, which none of us had ever seen before, with some scenes shot at Millbrook in 1966 when Timothy was in his absolute *prime*—virile, brilliant, glowing with intelligence, and just beautiful and vibrant . . . a perfect moment in his life captured on film. He was so casually articulate and presented his viewpoint with such clarity and conviction that surely anyone watching at any time who had never dropped acid would feel compelled to do so immediately. The charisma literally dripped off his body. Tim and a few of us were pretty stoned, and I was sitting behind him on his bed—in awe of this man and his work and this little part of his life I'd never seen, when I felt him shuddering and he leaned back on me with such force that I almost fell. . . . I just held him up as he cried, longing to give him back this moment on film—the youth, the beauty, the goals; to personally eradicate death's shadow spying on him over in the corner, waiting to rob him of his vision, his mind. It was the night I most hated his illness and the night I was properly introduced to Timothy's regret. It made me fully cherish every second I spent with him that much more.

STACY VALIS

Administrator, Warner Bros. Art Department

How I Met Tim: I entered Tim's world through my husband, Dean Chamberlain, and was probably one of the more unlikely candidates to become part of Tim's inner circle. I am not really what you'd call spontaneous or the life of the party. I had a very modest drug history. I am by no means a celebrity, and I'm convinced that had I met Tim any earlier in his life, he would have been friendly and polite and promptly forgotten me.

I came into a house of constant activity, both mental and physical, and was quickly drawn to the atmosphere of love generated by many of the people who lived with or frequently visited Tim. I became a sort of den mother. I cooked and cleaned and generally looked after household things and I found security in my role of supporting the people who were supporting Tim. As the days passed, I became more comfortable around everyone, including Tim, and I occasionally ventured out with Tim and the tribe to various social events—dinners, concerts, ceremonies. But as it drew closer to the time of Tim's passing, he began slowly to retreat from decades of public life and gradually started an inner journey, which allowed me to spend some reflective moments with him that will remain with me always. I think Tim and I connected at that time of his life because, given the choice, I will usually opt for conversation rather than other social activities, and in those final days he was much more inclined to sit and talk. I came to love and respect him so much that I wanted to learn as much as I could from him, and I valued every second I was given to be with him. As his physical health failed, he turned more exclusively to his intellectual self, and finally toward the realm of light and spirit.

The morning Tim passed—shortly after midnight on May 31—Dean and I went back to our house at around 6 A.M. to get some sleep. I dreamed that I saw Tim as if he had been drawn by William Blake—long, flowing white hair and beard, and intensely blue eyes, looking straight at me. I looked back at him and said, "You're so beautiful!" It was Tim as God spirit.

Lesson: For me, Tim's legacy transcends his popular image. I really didn't have much first- or even second-hand knowledge of Tim. I had seen him speak only once in the early 1990s and hadn't read his books; most of what I knew of him was what the media portrayed and, more recently, what Dean, a longtime Tim fan, imparted to me. What I came to realize was, when you looked at who Tim was apart from the LSD-guru and Hollywood-socialite performer tags, you found the fundamental Tim, the unwaveringly brave, honest, loving, tireless man with an unequaled work ethic, enthusiasm in the face of all adversities, and unconditional love and support for those of us fortunate enough to have orbited him. The way he approached his death underscored the lessons of his life. I can never again shirk, feel like maybe I've done enough when deep down I know I haven't, or evade truth without thinking of Tim and knowing I have to rise to a higher level. Those of us who knew Tim may say that we're only doing what he expected of us, but actually Tim was mirroring to us our own expectations, and his life and death gave us an example to follow to be able to live our lives as fully and honestly as he did.

Favorite Memory: One night Dean and I went to visit Tim and the house was unusually quiet. Everyone had gone out for a much-needed break, and Tim was alone in his room with Rosemary when we arrived. We spent the evening in conversation, Tim and Rosemary reminisced (much to Dean's and my delight, as we felt that we were being bestowed with a verbal draft of an amazing autobiography), and we eventually made our way into Tim's office. Tim turned his attention to various items on the desk and became involved in an elaborate numbering and referencing system for geography that my inferior brain scrambled to keep up with. At one point, Tim asked us to bring him a copy of his bibliography, a faithful and exhaustive volume compiled by archivist Michael Horowitz. Tim asked me the correct spelling of my name, and I noticed he began inscribing something on the title page of the bibliography. When he handed it to me, I saw that he had written, "To Stacy and Dean. Please memorize by heart (with a drawing of a smiling heart next to it). Love, Timothy Leary." I immediately thought of *Fahrenheit 451* and imagined that, had I been a character in it, I would become Tim's book.

I have another favorite memory too. The weekend before Tim died, Dean and I had volunteered to stay over at this house for two nights. On Saturday night, we finally convinced Tim to go to bed around midnight (no mean feat as his usual "bedtime" was 5 A.M., and he probably averaged two to three hours of sleep a night) and, as he hadn't slept the night before, he fell asleep soon thereafter. I slept on the bed next to him, and our beautiful friend Tara was close to his other side leaning onto the bed from a chair next to him and encircling him with her arms. Tim slept lightly and fitfully and frequently had to sit up due to a deep cough that plagued him. At one point, we were asleep and the phone rang. He and I looked at each other, a bit startled at being woken up by the ringing, and he nodded to me to answer the phone. It was Ram Dass, and he and Tim had a very cheerful, brief conversation during which Tim made some very funny remarks relating to his decreasing memory functions. He went back to sleep. I tried to do the same, and around 5 A.M. Tim woke up. I peered over at him with eyes burning from lack of sleep to see that Tara had gone and tried unsuccessfully to convince him that we should sleep a bit longer. As I knew would be the case, he wasn't having it, and the next thing I knew I was in the kitchen preparing us Tim's favorite instant coffee and carrying it out to a round table that had been the scene of many a lively gathering. We sat facing the window that overlooked the beautiful yard and watched as the sun was rising. The light was golden, and I remarked that it reminded me of the light in Greece. I asked if he had ever been to Greece, and that led us to speak of the time he lived in Italy. He began recounting his time there as if it had been yesterday, in great detail, painting a picture that allowed me to see his memory. After a while, we were quiet a moment, we looked at each other, and I said to him, "You've had an amazing life," to which he replied, factually and with no false modesty, "I *have* had an amazing life."

ROBERT ANTON WILSON

Author, philosopher, longtime collaborator with Tim Leary

Lesson: Nothing has meaning in itself, not even death; we give meaning to all events. In making death a personal celebration—keeping away from the agents of authoritarianism like the church, the state, and the AMA and designing his own passing—Tim taught his greatest lesson.

I learned not to fear death. I realize that we don't have to choose between Dylan Thomas's stark alternatives—to "go gently into that good night" or to "rage, rage against the dying of the light." Tim showed how you can laugh and party all the way, and that's the way I intend to go when my time comes.

Favorite Memory: I have hundreds and hundreds of favorite memories of Tim, but right now I guess my favorite *favorite* would be the email I got from him a month after his passing. It said: "Robert, how is everything? Greetings from the other side. . . . It's not what I expected. Nice, but crowded. . . . Hope you're well. Love, Timothy."

Of all Dr. Leary's jokes, I guess I will always treasure that one the most.

R.U. Sirius is cofounder and original editor-in-chief of the first cyberculture magazine, *Mondo 2000.* Recent books include *How to Mutate and Take Over the World: An Exploded Post-Novel* (Ballantine Books, 1996) and *Cyberpunk Handbook: The Real Cyberpunk Fakebook* (Random House, 1995). He's a regular columnist for *21•C* and *EYE-COM* and a frequent contributor to *ARTFORUM International, Mondo 2000,* and *Wired.* He lectures internationally about technology and popular culture and has been called "the wired visionary of psychic pandemonium" and "a head on the Mt. Rushmore of cyberculture."